D1390957

LITTLE PUFFERS

A Guide to Britain's Narrow Gauge & Miniature Railways 2006-2007

EDITOR
John Robinson

Second Edition

ACKNOWLEDGEMENTS

We were greatly impressed by the friendly and cooperative manner of the staff and helpers of the railways which we selected to appear in this book, and wish to thank them all for the help they have given. In addition we wish to thank Bob Budd (cover design) and Michael Robinson (page layouts) for their help.

Although we believe that the information contained in this guide is accurate at the time of going to press, we, and the Railways and Museums itemised, are unable to accept liability for any loss, damage, distress or injury suffered as a result of any inaccuracies. Furthermore, we and the Railways are unable to guarantee operating and opening times which may always be subject to cancellation without notice.

If you feel we should include other locations or information in future editions, please let us know so that we may give them consideration. We would like to thank you for buying this guide and wish you 'Happy Railway Travelling'!

John Robinson

EDITOR

Note: Further copies of Little Puffers and Still Steaming may be obtained, post free, from our address below or ordered on-line via our web site – www.stillsteaming.com

British Library Cataloguing in Publication Data
A catalogue record for this book is available from the British Library

ISBN-10:   1-86223-141-9
ISBN-13:   978-1-86223-141-2   (for use after January 2007)

Copyright © 2006, MARKSMAN PUBLICATIONS. (01472 696226)
72 St. Peter's Avenue, Cleethorpes, N.E. Lincolnshire, DN35 8HU, England

Manufactured in the UK by LPPS Ltd, Wellingborough, NN8 3PJ

FOREWORD

The photograph on the cover of this book was taken at the Heatherslaw Light Railway in Northumberland during August 2005. This railway is probably unique insofar as the 2 mile line is operated by Ford and Etal Estates and the steam loco uses sawmill offcuts as fuel!

Following the success of the 1st edition of Little Puffers, we have introduced no fewer than seventeen new sites in this edition. We have also fully updated all other entries and have included many new photographs making the book better than ever!

CONTENTS

RAILWAY LOCATOR MAP

The numbers shown on this map relate to the page numbers for each railway. Pages 3-5 contain an alphabetical listing of the railways featured in this guide. Please note that the markers on this map show the approximate location only.

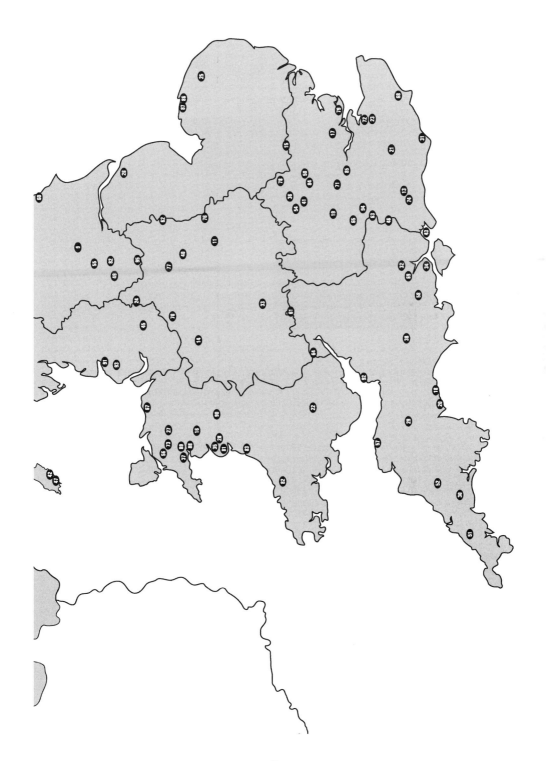

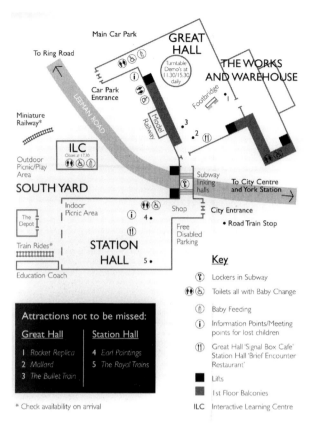

THE FRIENDS OF THE NATIONAL RAILWAY MUSEUM

This organisation was formed in 1977 to help conserve and operate railway exhibits that might otherwise have to wait many years before returning to public view. The organisation is run on a membership basis which imparts a number of privileges which include:

- the *NRM Review*, published quarterly, which keeps Friends in touch with events at the Museum, carries information about the National Collection locomotives, features articles of general railway interest and includes authorative reviews of videos and books.

- opportunities to work as a volunteer in the Museum.

- invitations to FNRM members meetings in York and London.

MEMBERSHIP DETAILS – Normal membership is valid for 12 months from date of registration.

Category	Rate
Ordinary	£20.00
Unwaged	£15.00
Junior (Under 18)	£10.00
Family/Couple	£30.00
Retired Couple	£22.50
Group	£35.00
Life (below 60)	£300.00
Life (60 and over)	£225.00
Life (retired couple)	£350.00
Life (family)	£450.00

Apply for membership to:

FNRM
National Railway Museum
Leeman Road
York
YO26 4XJ

Telephone (01904) 636874
e-mail fnrm@nmsi.ac.uk

Family Membership – is for a maximum of four persons, two or three of whom are under 18 years of age, residing at the same address

Retired Couple Membership – is for two persons aged 60 or over and not in employment.

NATIONAL RAILWAY MUSEUM

Address: National Railway Museum, Leeman Road, York YO26 4XJ **Telephone Nº**: (01904) 621261 **Year Formed**: 1975 **Location of Line**: York **Length of Line**: Short demonstration line	**Nº of Steam Locos**: 79 **Nº of Other Locos**: 37 **Approx Nº of Visitors P.A.**: 800,000 **Web site**: www.nrm.org.uk

GENERAL INFORMATION

Nearest Mainline Station: York (¼ mile)
Nearest Bus Station: York (¼ mile)
Car Parking: On site long stay car park
Coach Parking: On site – free to pre-booked groups
Souvenir Shop(s): Yes
Food & Drinks: Yes

SPECIAL INFORMATION

The Museum is the largest of its kind in the world, housing the Nation's collection of locomotives, carriages, uniforms, posters and an extensive photographic archive. Special events and exhibitions run throughout the year. The Museum is the home of the Mallard – the fastest steam locomotive in the world and Shinkansen, the only Bullet train outside of Japan.

OPERATING INFORMATION

Opening Times: Open daily 10.00am to 6.00pm (closed on 24th, 25th and 26th of December)
Steam Working: School holidays – please phone to confirm details
Prices: Free admission for all (excludes some Special events)
Phone (01904) 686263 for further details.

Detailed Directions by Car:
The Museum is located in the centre of York, just behind the Railway Station. It is clearly signposted from all approaches to York.

LOCOMOTION – THE NATIONAL RAILWAY MUSEUM AT SHILDON

Address: Locomotion, Shildon, County Durham   DL14 1PQ
Telephone N°: (01388) 777999
Year Formed: 2004
Location: Shildon, County Durham
Length of Line: Over ½ mile

N° of Steam Locos: 60 locomotives and other rail vehicles
Approx N° of Visitors P.A.: 60,000+
Gauge: Standard
Web site: www.locomotion.uk.com

GENERAL INFORMATION

Nearest Mainline Station: Shildon (adjacent)
Nearest Bus Station: Durham
Car Parking: Available on site
Coach Parking: Available on site
Souvenir Shop(s): Yes
Food & Drinks: Yes

SPECIAL INFORMATION

This extensive site is the first regional branch of the National Railway Museum and houses vehicles from the National Collection in a purpose-built 6,000 square-foot building.

OPERATING INFORMATION

Opening Times: Daily from 7th April 2006 to 31st October 2006 – 10.00am to 5.00pm. Also open from Wednesday to Sunday during the Winter – 10.00am to 4.00pm.
Steam Working: During the Summer School Holidays and on special event days – please phone to confirm details.
Prices: Free admission for all.

Detailed Directions by Car:
From All Parts: Exit the A1(M) at Junction 58 and take the A68 and the A6072 to Shildon. Follow the Brown tourist signs to Locomotion which is situated ¼ mile to the south-east of the Town Centre.

ABBEY PUMPING STATION

Address: Abbey Pumping Station Museum, Corporation Road, Leicester, LE4 5PX **Telephone N°**: (0116) 299-5111 **Year Formed**: 1980s **Location of Line**: Leicester **Length of Line**: 300 yards	**N° of Steam Locos**: 1 **N° of Other Locos**: 4 **N° of Members**: Approximately 80 **Annual Membership Fee**: £15.00 **Approx N° of Visitors P.A.**: 60,000 **Gauge**: 2 feet

GENERAL INFORMATION

Nearest Mainline Station: Leicester London Road (3 miles)
Nearest Bus Station: Leicester (1½ miles)
Car Parking: Available on site
Coach Parking: Available on site
Souvenir Shop(s): Yes
Food & Drinks: Available on special event days only

SPECIAL INFORMATION

The Museum is situated in the Abbey Pumping Station which, from 1891 to 1964 pumped Leicester's sewage to nearby treatment works. The Museum now collects and displays the industrial, technological and scientific heritage of Leicester and contains rare working examples of Woolf compound rotative beam engines which are in steam on selected days.

OPERATING INFORMATION

Opening Times: Monday to Wednesday and weekends from the beginning of February to the end of November. Open 11.00am – 4.30pm on weekdays and Saturdays and 1.00pm – 4.30pm on Sundays.
Steam Working: Selected special event days only. 2006 dates: 1st & 9th April; 6th May; 3rd June; 24th and 25th June; 1st July; 5th August; 2nd & 10th September; 7th October; 10th December
Prices: Adults £3.50 (Special event days only)
Concessions £2.00 (Special events only)
Family £7.00 (Special event days only)

Detailed Directions by Car:
From All Parts: The Museum is situated next to the National Space Centre, about 1 mile north of Leicester city centre near Beaumont Leys and Belgrave. Brown tourist signs with a distinctive rocket logo provide directions to the NSC from the arterial routes around Leicester and the Museum is nearby.

ALFORD VALLEY RAILWAY

Address: Alford Station, Main Street, Alford, Aberdeenshire AB33 8HH	**Nº of Steam Locos**: None at present
	Nº of Other Locos: 3
Telephone Nº: (01975) 562811	**Nº of Members**: Approximately 30
Year Formed: 1980	**Annual Membership Fee**: £6.00
Location of Line: Alford – Haughton Park	**Approx Nº of Visitors P.A.**: 19,500
Length of Line: 1 mile	**Gauge**: 2 feet

GENERAL INFORMATION

Nearest Mainline Station: Insch (10 miles)
Nearest Bus Station: Alford (200 yards)
Car Parking: Available on site
Coach Parking: Available on site
Souvenir Shop(s): Yes
Food & Drinks: No

SPECIAL INFORMATION

The Grampian Transport Museum is adjacent to the Railway and the Heritage Centre also has horse-drawn tractors and agricultural machinery.

OPERATING INFORMATION

Opening Times: Weekends in April, May and September. Open daily in June, July and August. Trains run from 1.00pm to 4.30pm
Steam Working: None at present
Prices: Adult Return £2.00
 Child Return £1.00

Web site: www.alfordvalleyrailway.org.uk

Detailed Directions by Car:
From All Parts: Alford is situated 25 miles west of Aberdeen on the Highland tourist route. Take the A944 to reach Alford.

AMBERLEY WORKING MUSEUM

Address: Amberley Working Museum, Amberley, Arundel BN18 9LT	**Nº of Steam Locos**: 3
Telephone Nº: (01798) 831370	**Nº of Other Locos**: 20+
Year Formed: 1979	**Nº of Members**: 300 volunteers
Location of Line: Amberley	**Annual Membership Fee**: £25.00
Length of Line: ¾ mile	**Approx Nº of Visitors P.A.**: 60,000
	Gauge: 2 feet

GENERAL INFORMATION

Nearest Mainline Station: Amberley (adjacent)
Nearest Bus Station: –
Car Parking: Free parking available on site
Coach Parking: Free parking available on site
Souvenir Shop(s): Yes
Food & Drinks: Yes

SPECIAL INFORMATION

Amberley Working Museum covers 36 acres of former chalk pits and consists of over 30 buildings containing hundreds of different exhibits.

The Railway is holding its annual Gala weekend on 8th and 9th July.

OPERATING INFORMATION

Opening Times: Wednesday to Sunday from 15th March to 29th October and also on Bank Holidays. Trains run from 10.00am to 5.30pm
Steam Working: Please phone for details.
Prices: Adult £8.20
  Child £5.00 (free for Under-5's)
  Family £23.00 (2 adults + 3 children)

Web site: www.amberleymuseum.co.uk

Detailed Directions by Car:
From All Parts: Amberley Working Museum is situated in West Sussex on the B2139 mid-way between Arundel and Storrington and is adjacent to Amberley Railway Station.

AMERTON RAILWAY

Address: Amerton Farm, Stow-by-Chartley, Staffordshire ST18 0LA	**Nº of Steam Locos**: 3
Telephone Nº: (01785) 850965	**Nº of Other Locos**: 7
Year Formed: 1991	**Nº of Members**: 45
Location: Amerton Farm	**Approx Nº of Visitors P.A.**: 30,000
Length of Line: Approximately 1 mile	**Gauge**: 2 feet
	Web site: www.amertonrailway.co.uk

GENERAL INFORMATION

Nearest Mainline Station: Stafford (8 miles)
Nearest Bus Station: Stafford (8 miles)
Car Parking: Free parking available on site
Coach Parking: Available by arrangement
Souvenir Shop(s): Yes
Food & Drinks: Yes

SPECIAL INFORMATION

The Railway is run by volunteers and the circuit was completed in 2002. The Summer Steam Gala will be held on 17th & 18th June.

OPERATING INFORMATION

Opening Times: Weekends from the end of March to the end of October and on Tuesdays & Thursdays during School Holidays. Also open for Santa Specials in December. Open from midday to 5.00pm
Steam Working: Sundays and Bank Holidays only.
Prices: Adult £1.50
Child £1.00
Concession £1.20
Family Ticket £4.00

Detailed Directions by Car:
Amerton is located on the A518, 1 mile from the junction with the A51 – Amerton Farm is signposted at the junction. The Railway is located approximately 8 miles from Junction 14 of the M6.

AUDLEY END STEAM RAILWAY

Address: Audley End, Saffron Walden, Essex **Telephone Nº**: (01799) 541354 **Year Formed**: 1964 **Location of Line**: Opposite Audley End House, Saffron Walden	**Length of Line**: 1½ miles **Nº of Steam Locos**: 6 **Nº of Other Locos**: 3 **Nº of Members**: None **Approx Nº of Visitors P.A.**: 42,000 **Gauge**: 10¼ inches **Web site**: www.audley-end-railway.co.uk

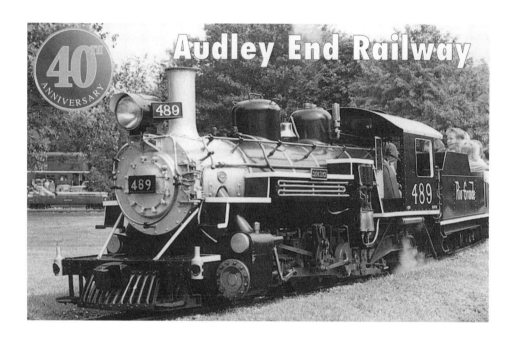

GENERAL INFORMATION

Nearest Mainline Station: Audley End (1 mile)
Nearest Bus Station: Saffron Walden (1 mile)
Car Parking: Available on site
Coach Parking: Available on site
Souvenir Shop(s): Yes
Food & Drinks: Snacks available

SPECIAL INFORMATION

Audley End Steam Railway is Lord Braybrooke's private miniature railway situated just next to Audley End House, an English Heritage site. Private parties can be catered for outside of normal running hours.

OPERATING INFORMATION

Opening Times: Weekends from Easter to the end of October and also daily during School Holidays. Also Santa Specials in December. Trains run from 2.00pm (11.00am on Bank Holidays).
Steam Working: Sundays only
Prices: Adult Return £2.50
Child Return £1.50
Santa Specials £3.50

Detailed Directions by Car:
Exit the M11 at Junction 10 if southbound or Junction 9 if northbound and follow the signs for Audley End House. The railway is situated just across the road from Audley End House.

BALA LAKE RAILWAY

Address: Bala Lake Railway, Llanuwchllyn, Gwynedd, LL23 7DD	**N° of Steam Locos**: 5 (all are not in
Telephone N°: (01678) 540666	**N° of Other Locos**: 3 working order)
Year Formed: 1972	**N° of Members**: –
Location of Line: Llanuwchllyn to Bala	**Approx N° of Visitors P.A.**: 20,000
Length of Line: 4½ miles	**Gauge**: 1 foot 11 five-eighth inches
	Web site: www.bala-lake-railway.co.uk

GENERAL INFORMATION

Nearest Mainline Station: Wrexham (40 miles)
Nearest Bus Station: Wrexham (40 miles)
Car Parking: Adequate parking in Llanuwchllyn
Coach Parking: At Llanuwchllyn or in Bala Town Centre
Souvenir Shop(s): Yes
Food & Drinks: Yes – unlicensed!

SPECIAL INFORMATION

Bala Lake Railway is a narrow-gauge railway which follows 4½ miles of the former Ruabon to Barmouth G.W.R. line.

OPERATING INFORMATION

Opening Times: 8th April to 1st October.
Steam Working: All advertised services are steam hauled. Trains run from 11.15am to 4.00pm.
Prices: Adult Single £4.50; Return £7.00
Child Single £2.00; Return £3.00
Senior Citizen Return £6.50
Family Tickets (Return): £8.50 (1 Adult + 1 Child); £17.00 (2 Adults + 2 Children). Additional Children are £2.00 each. Under 5's and dogs travel free of charge!

Detailed Directions by Car:
From All Parts: The railway is situated off the A494 Bala to Dolgellau road which is accessible from the national motorways via the A5 or A55.

BARLEYLANDS MINIATURE RAILWAY

Address: Barleylands, Barleylands Road, Billericay, Essex CM11 2UD
Telephone Nº: (01268) 290229
Year Formed: 1989
Location of Line: 3 miles from Billericay
Length of Line: ½ mile
Web site: www.barleylands.co.uk

Nº of Steam Locos: 5
Nº of Other Locos: 2
Nº of Members: None
Annual Membership Fee: –
Approx Nº of Visitors P.A.: 10,000+
Gauge: 7¼ inches

GENERAL INFORMATION

Nearest Mainline Station: Billericay or Basildon
Nearest Bus Station: Billericay or Basildon
Car Parking: Available on site
Coach Parking: Available on site
Souvenir Shop(s): Yes
Food & Drinks: Yes

SPECIAL INFORMATION

The Railway is located in the Barleylands Craft Village and Farm Centre which has a wide range of attractions for all ages. The railway is commercially operated but volunteers help to operate and maintain the steam engines.

OPERATING INFORMATION

Opening Times: Daily from March to October with Santa Specials in December.
Steam Working: Sundays and Bank Holidays then daily (except Saturdays) from 14th to 31st August and October Half-Term week. Also at a number of other special events throughout the year. Please phone the railway to confirm all running dates.
Prices: £1.00 Return (all ages) when Diesel-hauled
£1.50 Return (all ages) when Steam-hauled

Detailed Directions by Car:
From M25: Exit at J29 onto A127 (Southend bound) and follow the brown Tourist Information signs for Farm Museum; From the A12: Take the B1007 Billericay junction, towards Stock and follow the brown Tourist Information signs for Farm Museum.

BEER HEIGHTS LIGHT RAILWAY

Address: Pecorama, Beer, East Devon, EX12 3NA
Telephone Nº: (01297) 21542
Year Formed: 1975
Location of Line: Beer, East Devon
Length of Line: 1 mile

Nº of Steam Locos: 5 at present
Nº of Other Locos: 1
Nº of Members: –
Approx Nº of Visitors P.A.: 60,000
Gauge: 7¼ inches
Web site: www.peco-uk.com

GENERAL INFORMATION

Nearest Mainline Station: Axminster
Nearest Bus Station: Beer
Car Parking: Available on site
Coach Parking: Available on site
Souvenir Shop(s): Yes
Food & Drinks: Licensed restaurant on site

SPECIAL INFORMATION

In addition to the Railway, Pecorama features a Model Railway Exhibition, childrens activity areas and extensive gardens.

OPERATING INFORMATION

Opening Times: Weekdays 10.00am to 5.30pm and Saturdays 10.00am to 1.00pm from Easter to the end of October. Also open on Sundays from Whitsun to the start of September from 10.00am to 5.30pm
Steam Working: Daily
Prices: Adult £5.75
    Child £3.80 (Under-4s free of charge)
    Senior Citizens £5.25 (Over-80s free)
Entrance to Pecorama includes one ride on the railway in the price.

Detailed Directions by Car:
From All Parts: Take the A3052 to Beer, turn onto the B3174 and follow the Brown Tourist signs for Pecorama.

Bekonscot Light Railway

Address: Bekonscot Model Village, Warwick Road, Beaconsfield, Bucks, HP9 2PL	**N° of Steam Locos**: None at present
	N° of Other Locos: 3
	N° of Members: –
Telephone N°: (01494) 672919	**Approx N° of Visitors P.A.**: 180,000
Year Formed: 2001	**Gauge**: 7¼ inches
Location of Line: Beaconsfield, Bucks.	**Web site**: www.bekonscot.co.uk
Length of Line: 400 yards	

GENERAL INFORMATION

Nearest Mainline Station: Beaconsfield (5 minutes walk)
Nearest Bus Station: High Wycombe
Car Parking: Available on site
Coach Parking: Available on site
Souvenir Shop(s): Yes
Food & Drinks: Available

SPECIAL INFORMATION

The Railway is situated in Bekonscot Model Village, a 1½ acre miniature landscape of fields, farms, castles, churches, woods and lakes which also contains a model railway.

OPERATING INFORMATION

Opening Times: Daily from mid-February to the end of October. Open 10.00am to 5.00pm.
Steam Working: None at present
Prices: Adult £5.80
Child £3.80
Family Ticket £17.60
Senior Citizen £4.20

Detailed Directions by Car:
From All Parts: Exit the M40 at Junction 2 taking the A355 then follow the signs for the "Model Village".

BICTON WOODLAND RAILWAY

Address: Bicton Woodland Railway, Bicton Park Botanical Gardens, East Budleigh, Budleigh Salterton EX9 7OP
Telephone Nº: (01395) 568465
Year Formed: 1963
Location of Line: Bicton Gardens
Length of Line: 1½ miles

Nº of Steam Locos: None at present
Nº of Other Locos: 3
Nº of Members: 15,000
Annual Membership Fee: £12.00
Approx Nº of Visitors P.A.: 300,000
Gauge: 1 foot 6 inches
Web site: www.bictongardens.co.uk

GENERAL INFORMATION

Nearest Railtrack Station: Exmouth (6 miles)
Nearest Bus Station: Exeter (14 miles)
Car Parking: Free parking at site
Coach Parking: Free parking at site
Souvenir Shop(s): Yes
Food & Drinks: Yes

SPECIAL INFORMATION

The railway runs through the grounds of Bicton Park Botanical Gardens which span over 60 acres.

OPERATING INFORMATION

Opening Times: Daily 10.00am to 6.00pm during the Summer and 10.00am to 5.00pm during the Winter. Closed on Christmas Day and Boxing Day.
Steam Working: None at present
Entrance Fee: Adult £5.95
                                 Child/Senior Citizen £4.95
                                 Family £19.95
Note: There is an additional charge of £1.30 per person for train rides. Under-3s ride for free.

Detailed Directions by Car:
From All Parts: Exit the M5 motorway at Exeter services, Junction 30 and follow the brown tourist signs to Bicton Park.

BOLEBROKE CASTLE & LAKES STEAM RAILWAY

Address: Bolebroke Castle, Edenbridge Road, Hartfield, East Sussex TN7 4JJ	**No of Steam Locos:** 7
Telephone No: (01892) 770061	**No of Other Locos:** 8
Year Formed: 1984	**No of Members:** Approximately 36
Location of Line: Bolebroke Castle	**Annual Membership Fee:** £15.00
Length of Line: ½ mile	**Approx No of Visitors P.A.:** –
	Gauge: 7¼ inches

GENERAL INFORMATION
Nearest Mainline Station: Tunbridge Wells
Nearest Bus Station: Hartfield
Car Parking: Available on site
Coach Parking: Available on site
Souvenir Shop(s): Yes
Food & Drinks: Yes

SPECIAL INFORMATION
The Railway runs around a lake situated in the grounds of a historic 15th Century Castle. Entrance to the castle is restricted so please phone for details of opening times.

OPERATING INFORMATION
Opening Times: Weekends from April to October and daily during the School holidays.
Steam Working: Some Sundays – phone for details
Prices: Admission to the grounds of the castle is free of charge. Admission prices for the castle itself are:
    Adult £5.00
    Child £2.50
    Senior Citizen £4.50

Detailed Directions by Car:
From All Parts: Take the A264 from Tunbridge Wells towards East Grinstead and turn off for Hartfield on either the B2110 (via Groombridge) or the B2026. Follow signs for Bolebroke Castle for the railway.

BRECON MOUNTAIN RAILWAY

Address: Pant Station, Dowlais, Merthyr Tydfil CF48 2UP
Telephone Nº: (01685) 722988
Year Formed: 1980
Location of Line: North of Merthyr Tydfil – 1 mile from the A465
Gauge: 1 foot 11¾ inches

Length of Line: 5 miles (3½ in service)
Nº of Steam Locos: 8
Nº of Other Locos: 1
Nº of Members: –
Annual Membership Fee: –
Approx Nº of Visitors P.A.: 75,000
Web site: www.breconmountainrailway.co.uk

GENERAL INFORMATION

Nearest Mainline Station: Merthyr Tydfil (3 miles)
Nearest Bus Station: Merthyr Tydfil (3 miles)
Car Parking: Available at Pant Station
Coach Parking: Available at Pant Station
Souvenir Shop(s): Yes
Food & Drinks: Yes – including licensed restaurant

SPECIAL INFORMATION

It is possible to take a break before the return journey at Pontsticill to have a picnic, take a forest walk or visit the lakeside snackbar.

OPERATING INFORMATION

Opening Times: Daily from 25th March to 29th October. Closed on some Mondays and Fridays in April, May, September and October.
Steam Working: 11.00am to 5.15pm
Prices: Adult Return £8.50
Child Return (15 and under) £4.25
Senior Citizen Return £7.75
Dogs or Bicycles £2.00
Family Rate – The first two children can travel for £3.00 each when accompanied by an adult.

Detailed Directions by Car:
Exit the M4 at Junction 32 and take the A470 to Merthyr Tydfil. Go onto the A465 and follow the brown tourist signs for the railway.

BREDGAR & WORMSHILL LIGHT RAILWAY

Address: The Warren, Bredgar, near Sittingbourne, Kent ME9 8AT	**N° of Steam Locos:** 13
Telephone N°: (01622) 884254	**N° of Other Locos:** 1
Year Formed: 1972	**N° of Members:** –
Location of Line: 1 mile south of Bredgar	**Annual Membership Fee:** –
Gauge: 2 feet	**Approx N° of Visitors P.A.:** 7,000
Length of Line: ¾ mile	**Web site:** www.bwlr.co.uk

GENERAL INFORMATION

Nearest Mainline Station:
Hollingbourne (3 miles) or Sittingbourne (5 miles)
Nearest Bus Station: Sittingbourne
Car Parking: 500 spaces available – free parking
Coach Parking: Free parking available by appointment
Souvenir Shop(s): Yes
Food & Drinks: Yes

SPECIAL INFORMATION

A small but beautiful railway in rural Kent. The railway also has other attractions including a Model Railway, Traction Engines, a working Beam Engine, Vintage cars, a Locomotive Shed, a picnic site and woodland walks.

OPERATING INFORMATION

Opening Times: Open on the first Sunday of the month from May to October. Open from 10.30am to 5.00pm
Steam Working: 11.00am to 4.30pm
Prices: Adult £6.00   Child £3.00

Detailed Directions by Car:
Take the M20 and exit at Junction 8 (Leeds Castle exit). Travel 4½ miles due north through Hollingbourne. The Railway is situated a little over 1 mile south of Bredgar village.

BROOKSIDE MINIATURE RAILWAY

Address: Macclesfield Road (A523), Poynton, Cheshire SK12 1BY
Telephone Nº: (01625) 872919
Year Formed: 1989
Location: Brookside Garden Centre
Length of Line: Approximately ½ mile

Nº of Steam Locos: 5
Nº of Other Locos: 3
Nº of Members: –
Approx Nº of Visitors P.A.: 120,000
Gauge: 7¼ inches
Web: www.brookside-miniature-railway.co.uk

GENERAL INFORMATION

Nearest Mainline Station: Poynton and Hazel Grove (both 1 mile)
Nearest Bus Station: Stockport (5 miles).
Car Parking: 400 spaces available on site
Coach Parking: 2 spaces available
Souvenir Shop(s): Yes
Food & Drinks: Yes

SPECIAL INFORMATION

The Railway runs through the grounds of the Brookside Garden Centre. There is also an extensive collection of Railwayana on display.

OPERATING INFORMATION

Opening Times: Railway is open weekends and Bank Holidays plus Wednesdays from March to September. Open every day in July and August. Trains usually run from 10.45am to 4.30pm but only until 4.00pm from November to February.
Steam Working: Weekends and Bank Holidays only
Prices: Adult £1.00 per ride (10 ride tickets £8.00)
Child £1.00 per ride (10 ride tickets £8.00)
Note: Under-2s ride for free

Detailed Directions by Car:
From the North: Exit the M60 at Junction 1 in Stockport and take the A6 (signposted Buxton). Upon reaching Hazel Grove, take the A523 to Poynton. Follow the brown tourist signs for the Railway; From the West: Exit the M56 at Junction 6 signposted Wilmslow and continue to Poynton. Follow the brown signs for the Railway; From the South: Exit the M6 at Junction 18 for Holmes Chapel. Follow the signs to Wilmslow, then as from the West; From the East: Follow the A6 to Hazel Grove, then as from the North.

BURE VALLEY RAILWAY

Address: Aylsham Station, Norwich Road, Aylsham, Norfolk NR11 6BW	**N° of Steam Locos**: 5
Telephone N°: (01263) 733858	**N° of Other Locos**: 3
Year Formed: 1989	**Approx N° of Visitors P.A.**: 127,000
Location of Line: Between Aylsham and Wroxham	**Gauge**: 15 inches
Length of Line: 9 miles	**Web Site**: www.bvrw.co.uk
	e-mail: info@bvrw.co.uk

GENERAL INFORMATION

Nearest Mainline Station: Wroxham (adjacent)
Nearest Bus Station: Aylsham (bus passes station)
Car Parking: Free parking at Aylsham & Wroxham Stations
Coach Parking: As above
Souvenir Shop(s): Yes at both Stations
Food & Drinks: Yes (also a Restaurant at Aylsham)

SPECIAL INFORMATION

Boat trains connect at Wroxham with a 1½ hour cruise on the Norfolk Broads. Steam Locomotive driving courses are available in off-peak periods. Some carriages are able to carry wheelchairs.

OPERATING INFORMATION

Opening Times: The station at Aylsham is open daily. Trains run on various dates from 11th February to 29th October. Daily from 1st April to 24th September. Trains run from 9.30am to 6.15pm during high season. Open for Santa Specials on dates in December – phone for further details.
Steam Working: Most trains are steam hauled
Prices: Adult Return £9.50   (Single £6.50)
  Child Return £5.50   (Single £4.50)
  Senior Cit. Return £9.00   (Single £6.00)
  Family Return £27.00 (2 adult + 2 child)
Party discounts are available for groups of 20 or more if booked in advance.

Detailed Directions by Car:
From Norwich: Aylsham Station is situated midway between Norwich and Cromer on the A140 – follow the Aylsham Town Centre signs. Wroxham Station is adjacent to the Wroxham British Rail Station – take the A1151 from Norwich; From King's Lynn: Take the A148 and B1354 to reach Aylsham Station.

CLEETHORPES COAST LIGHT RAILWAY

Address: King's Road, Cleethorpes, North East Lincolnshire DN35 0AG	**Nº of Steam Locos:** 7
Telephone Nº: (01472) 604657	**Nº of Other Locos:** 4
Year Formed: 1948	**Nº of Members:** 65
Location of Line: Lakeside Park & Marine embankment along Cleethorpes seafront	**Annual Membership Fee:** Adult £11.00
	Approx Nº of Visitors P.A.: 106,000
	Gauge: 15 inches
Length of Line: 1 mile	**Web:** www.cleethorpescoastlightrailway.co.uk

GENERAL INFORMATION

Nearest Mainline Station: Cleethorpes (1 mile)
Nearest Bus Stop: Meridian Point (opposite)
Car Parking: Boating Lake car park – 500 spaces (fee charged)
Coach Parking: As above
Souvenir Shop(s): Yes
Food & Drinks: Brief Encounters Tearoom on Lakeside Station

SPECIAL INFORMATION

The Sutton Collection Museum opened in May 2004.

OPERATING INFORMATION

Opening Times: Open daily from 9th to 18th April then daily from 1st May to 5th September. Open during weekends, Bank holidays and school holidays at all other times. Open 11.00am to dusk in Winter, 6.00pm in Summer.
Steam Working: Weekends throughout the year
Prices: Adult Return £2.50 (Single £2.00)
　　　　　Child Return £2.00 (Single £1.70)
　　　　　Family Return £8.00

Detailed Directions by Car:
Take the M180 to the A180 and continue to its' end. Follow signs for Cleethorpes. The Railway is situated along Cleethorpes seafront 1 mile south of the Pier. Look for the brown Railway Engine tourist signs and the main station is adjacent to the Leisure Centre.

CONWY VALLEY RAILWAY MUSEUM

Address: Old Goods Yard, Betws-y-Coed, Conwy, North Wales LL24 0AL	**Nº of Steam Locos:** 4
	Nº of Other Locos: 2
Telephone Nº: (01690) 710568	**Nº of Members:** –
Year Formed: 1983	**Annual Membership Fee:** –
Location of Line: Betws-y-Coed	**Approx Nº of Visitors P.A.:** 50,000
Length of Line: One and an eighth miles	**Gauge:** 7¼ inches and 15 inches

GENERAL INFORMATION

Nearest Mainline Station: Betws-y-Coed (20 yards)
Nearest Bus Station: 40 yards
Car Parking: Car park at site
Coach Parking: Car park at site
Souvenir Shop(s): Yes
Food & Drinks: Yes – Buffet Coach Cafe

SPECIAL INFORMATION

The Museum houses the unique 3D dioramas by the late Jack Nelson. Also the ¼ size steam loco 'Britannia'. The Railway now has two new Isle of Man locos – "Douglas" and "Dragonfly".

OPERATING INFORMATION

Opening Times: Daily from 10.00am to 5.30pm.
Trains Working: Daily from 10.15am
Prices: Adult – £1.50 museum entry;
Train rides £1.50; Tram rides £1.00
Child/Senior Citizen – £1.00 museum entry;
Train rides £1.50; Tram rides £1.00
Family tickets – £4.00

Detailed Directions by Car:
From Midlands & South: Take M54/M6 onto the A5 and into Betws-y-Coed; From Other Parts: Take the A55 coast road then the A470 to Betws-y-Coed. The museum is located by the Mainline Station directly off the A5.

THE CORRIS RAILWAY

Address: Station Yard, Corris,
Machynlleth, Mid Wales   SY20 9SH
Telephone Nº: (01654) 761303
Year Formed: 1966
Location of Line: Corris to Maespoeth,
Mid Wales
Length of Line: ¾ mile

Nº of Steam Locos: 1
Nº of Other Locos: 1
Nº of Members: 500
Annual Membership Fee: £15.00 (adult)
Approx Nº of Visitors P.A.: 7,000
Gauge: 2 feet 3 inches
Web site: www.corris.co.uk

GENERAL INFORMATION

Nearest Mainline Station: Machynlleth (5 miles)
Nearest Bus Station: Machynlleth (5 miles)
Car Parking: Available on site and also at the Corris Craft Centre (500 yards)
Coach Parking: Corris Craft Centre (please pre-book if visiting)
Souvenir Shop(s): Yes
Food & Drinks: Yes

SPECIAL INFORMATION

The Corris Railway Society was formed in 1966 and the line itself dates back to 1859. The Railway's new-build steam loco was delivered in the Spring of 2005.

OPERATING INFORMATION

Opening Times: Open during Easter week and weekends in May. Daily from June to the end of September and also during October school holidays. 10.30am to 5.30pm.
Steam Working: Please phone for details.
Prices: Adult Return £4.00
              Child/Senior Citizen Return £2.00

Detailed Directions by Car:
From All Parts: Corris is situated off the A487 trunk road, five miles north of Machynlleth and 11 miles south of Dolgellau. Turn off the trunk road at the Braichgoch Hotel and the Station Yard is the 2nd turn of the right as you enter the village, just past the Holy Trinity Church.

DEVON RAILWAY CENTRE

Address: Bickleigh, Tiverton, Devon, EX16 8RG **Telephone Nº**: (01884) 855671 **Year Formed**: 1997 **Location of Line**: Bickleigh, Devon **Length of Line**: ½ mile (2 foot and 7¼ inch gauges); 200 yards (Standard gauge)	**Nº of Steam Locos**: 3 **Nº of Other Locos**: 15 **Nº of Members**: None **Approx Nº of Visitors P.A.**: – **Gauge**: 2 feet, 7¼ inches and Standard **Web site**: www.devonrailwaycentre.co.uk

GENERAL INFORMATION

Nearest Mainline Station: Exeter
Nearest Bus Station: Tiverton (Route 55)
Car Parking: Available on site
Coach Parking: Available on site
Souvenir Shop(s): Yes
Food & Drinks: Yes

SPECIAL INFORMATION

Devon Railway Centre has passenger carrying lines and also features a large model railway exhibition with 15 working layouts. This is all centred around a genuine Victorian G.W.R. Station.

OPERATING INFORMATION

Opening Times: Daily 8th–23rd April then 27th May to 10th September & 21st–29th October. Closed Mondays during June. Open Wednesday to Friday & Weekends from 3rd–27th May and 13th September to 1st October. Open during Weekends in October and May Bank Holiday weekend. Open from 10.30am until 5.00pm.
Steam Working: Trains may be steam or diesel hauled so please phone for further information.
Prices: Adult £4.70   Child £3.70
           Senior Citizen £3.95   Family £14.60
Admission includes unlimited train rides and access to the model railways and museum.

Detailed Directions by Car:
From All Parts: Devon Railway Centre is situated adjacent to the famous Bickleigh Bridge, just off the A396 Exeter to Tiverton road (3 miles from Tiverton and 8 miles from Exeter).

DOBWALLS FAMILY ADVENTURE PARK

Address: Dobwalls Family Adventure Park, near Liskeard, Cornwall PL14 6HB	**N⁰ of Steam Locos**: 6
Telephone N⁰: (01579) 320325/321129	**N⁰ of Other Locos**: 4
Year Formed: 1970	**N⁰ of Members**: –
Location of Line: Near Liskeard, Cornwall	**Annual Membership Fee**: –
Length of Line: 2 × 1 mile tracks	**Gauge**: 7¼ inches
	Web site: www.dobwallsadventurepark.co.uk

GENERAL INFORMATION

Nearest Mainline Station: Liskeard (3 miles)
Nearest Bus Station: Most National Express Coaches travel through Dobwalls.
Car Parking: Ample parking available at site
Coach Parking: Large coach park available
Souvenir Shop(s): Yes
Food & Drinks: Yes

SPECIAL INFORMATION

Formerly known as the Forest Railroad Park, Dobwalls has a large number of other attractions including many for children. There is also an art gallery.

OPERATING INFORMATION

Opening Times: Open most days from Easter until the end of October. Opens from 10.30am to 5.00pm.
Steam Working: All days when open
Prices: Children under the age of 2 – Free
Single person ticket – £7.75
Family ticket (2 people) – £15.50
Family ticket (3 people) – £23.25
Family ticket (4 people) – £31.00
Disabled & Senior Citizens – £5.00
SuperSaver (weekends after 2.00pm) – £5.00
Group Price (20 people or more) – £3.50 per person

Detailed Directions by Car:
From All Parts: Dobwalls Family Adventure Park is situated just off the A38 at Dobwalls village, 3 miles from Liskeard.

EASTBOURNE MINIATURE STEAM RAILWAY

Address: Lottbridge Drove, Eastbourne, East Sussex BN23 6NS	**Nº of Steam Locos**: 6
Telephone Nº: (01323) 520229	**Nº of Other Locos**: 3
Year Formed: 1992	**Nº of Members**: –
Location of Line: Eastbourne	**Approx Nº of Visitors P.A.**: –
Length of Line: 1 mile	**Gauge**: 7¼ inches
	Web site: www.emsr.co.uk

GENERAL INFORMATION

Nearest Mainline Station: Eastbourne (2 miles)
Nearest Bus Station: Eastbourne (2 miles)
Car Parking: Free parking on site
Coach Parking: Free parking on site
Souvenir Shop(s): Yes
Food & Drinks: Yes

SPECIAL INFORMATION

The Railway site also has many other attractions including model railways, an adventure playground, nature walk, maze, picnic area and a Cafe.

OPERATING INFORMATION

Opening Times: Open 10.00am to 5.00pm daily from 1st April until 1st October. Also special events on Easter Sunday.
Steam Working: Weekends, Bank Holidays and during School Holidays. Diesel at other times.
Prices: Adult £4.45
Child £3.95 (2 years and under free)
Family Tickets £16.00
(2 adults + 2 children)

Detailed Directions by Car:
From All Parts: Take the A22 new road to Eastbourne then follow the Brown tourist signs for the 'Mini Railway'.

EASTLEIGH LAKESIDE STEAM RAILWAY

Address: Lakeside Country Park, Wide Lane, Eastleigh, Hants. SO50 5PE	**Nº of Steam Locos**: 13
Telephone Nº: (023) 8061-2020	**Nº of Other Locos**: 3
Year Formed: 1992	**Nº of Members**: –
Location: Opposite Southampton airport	**Approx Nº of Visitors P.A.**: 70,000
Length of Line: 1¼ miles	**Gauge**: 10¼ inches and 7¼ inches
	Web site: www.steamtrain.co.uk

GENERAL INFORMATION

Nearest Mainline Station: Southampton Airport (Parkway) (¼ mile)
Nearest Bus Station: Eastleigh (1½ miles)
Car Parking: Free parking available on site
Coach Parking: Free parking available on site
Souvenir Shop(s): Yes
Food & Drinks: Cafe open every day of the year

SPECIAL INFORMATION

The railway also has a playground and picnic area overlooking the lakes.

OPERATING INFORMATION

Opening Times: Weekends throughout the year and daily during July, August and September plus all school holidays. Open 10.30am to 4.15pm.
Santa Specials run on some dates in December.
Steam Working: As above
Prices: Standard Class Single £1.30; Return £2.00
First Class Single £1.50;   Return £2.50
3 rides per person – Standard £4.00;   First £5.00
Annual season tickets are available. Children under the age of 2 years ride free of charge.

Detailed Directions by Car:
From All Parts: Exit the M27 at Junction 5 and take the A335 to Eastleigh. The Railway is situated ¼ mile past Southampton Airport Station on the left hand side of the A335.

EVESHAM VALE LIGHT RAILWAY

Address: Evesham Country Park,
Twyford, Evesham WR11 4TP
Telephone Nº: (01386) 422282
Year Formed: 2002
Location of Line: 1 mile north of Evesham
Length of Line: 1¼ miles

Nº of Steam Locos: 5
Nº of Other Locos: 3
Nº of Members: None
Approx Nº of Visitors P.A.: 50,000
Gauge: 15 inches
Web site: www.evlr.co.uk

GENERAL INFORMATION

Nearest Mainline Station: Evesham (1 mile)
Nearest Bus Station: Evesham (1½ miles)
Car Parking: Available in the Country Park
Coach Parking: Available in the Country Park
Souvenir Shop(s): Yes
Food & Drinks: Restaurant at the Garden Centre

SPECIAL INFORMATION

The railway is situated within the 130 acre Evesham
Country Park which has apple orchards and picnic
areas overlooking the picturesque Vale of Evesham.

OPERATING INFORMATION

Opening Times: Open at weekends throughout the
year and daily during school holidays. Trains run
from 10.30am to 5.00pm. Please phone for further
details.
Steam Working: Daily when trains are running
Prices: Adult Return £1.80
Child Return £1.20
Senior Citizen Return £1.50

Detailed Directions by Car:
From the North: Exit the M42 at Junction 3 and take the A435 towards Alcester then the A46 to Evesham; From
the South: Exit the M5 at Junction 9 and take the A46 to Evesham; From the West: Exit the M5 at Junction 7 and
take the A44 to Evesham; From the East: Take the A44 from Oxford to Evesham. Upon reaching Evesham, follow
the Brown tourist signs for Evesham Country Park and the railway.

EXBURY GARDENS RAILWAY

Address: Exbury Gardens, Exbury, Near Southampton SO45 1AZ	**Nº of Steam Locos**: 2
Telephone Nº: (02380) 891203	**Nº of Other Locos**: 1
Year Formed: 2001	**Nº of Members**: None
Location of Line: Exbury	**Approx Nº of Visitors P.A.**: 55,000
Length of Line: 1½ miles	**Gauge**: 12¼ inches
	Web site: www.exbury.co.uk

GENERAL INFORMATION

Nearest Mainline Station: Brockenhurst (8 miles)
Nearest Bus Station: Southampton (12 miles)
Car Parking: Free parking available on site
Coach Parking: Free parking available on site
Souvenir Shop(s): Yes
Food & Drinks: Available

SPECIAL INFORMATION

The railway is located in the world famous Rothschild Azalea and Rhododendron gardens at Exbury in the New Forest. Footplate Experience days are available and the Engine Shed is licensed to host Civil Weddings!

OPERATING INFORMATION

Opening Times: Daily from the 1st March to 5th November. Also open for Santa Specials on 9th, 10th, 16th, 17th, 21st & 22nd December. Open from 10.00am to 5.30pm (or dusk if earlier)
Steam Working: Every running day from 11.00am.
Prices: Adult Return £2.50 – £3.00
          Child Return £2.50 – £3.00

Detailed Directions by Car:
Exit the M27 at Junction 2 and take the A326 to Dibden. Follow signs for Exbury.

FAIRBOURNE & BARMOUTH RAILWAY

Address: Beach Road, Fairbourne, Dolgellau, Gwynedd LL38 2EX
Telephone Nº: (01341) 250362
Year Formed: 1947
Location of Line: On A493 between Tywyn & Dolgellau
Length of Line: 2¼ miles

Nº of Steam Locos: 4
Nº of Other Locos: 2
Nº of Members: 87
Annual Membership Fee: £8.00
Approx Nº of Visitors P.A.: 25,000
Gauge: 12¼ inches
Web Site: www.fairbournerailway.com

GENERAL INFORMATION

Nearest Mainline Station: Fairbourne (adjacent)
Nearest Bus Station: Fairbourne (adjacent)
Car Parking: Available in Mainline station car park
Coach Parking: Pay & Display car park 300 yards (the Railway will re-imburse car parking charges for party bookings)
Souvenir Shop(s): Yes
Food & Drinks: Yes – Tea room at Fairbourne, Cafe at Porth Penrhyn Terminus

SPECIAL INFORMATION

There is a connecting ferry service (passenger only) to Barmouth from Porth Penrhyn Terminus.

OPERATING INFORMATION

Opening Times: Open 1st & 2nd April. Daily from 8th April to 24th September (closed on Fridays except from mid-July to the end of August). Also open most weekends in October then 21st to 29th October (but not 27th October). Santa Specials run on 9th and 10th December at 1.30pm.
Steam Working: 11.30am to 3.10pm for normal service. At peak times 10.40am to 4.20pm.
Prices: Adult Return £6.90
Child Return £3.90
Family £17.50 (2 adults + up to 3 children)
Senior Citizen Return £5.80

Detailed Directions by Car:
From North & East Wales: Follow Dolgellau signs, turn left onto A493 towards Tywyn. The turn-off for Fairbourne is located 9 miles south west of Dolgellau; From South Wales: Follow signs for Machynlleth, then follow A487 towards Dolgellau. Then take A493 towards Fairbourne.

FANCOTT MINIATURE RAILWAY

Address: Fancott Miniature Railway, Fancott, near Toddington, Bedfordshire
Telephone Nº: (01525) 872366
Year Formed: 1996
Location of Line: The Fancott Pub, near Toddington, Bedfordshire
Length of Line: ¼ mile

Nº of Steam Locos: 0
Nº of Other Locos: 3
Nº of Members: 8
Annual Membership Fee: £30.00
Approx Nº of Visitors P.A.: 10,000
Gauge: 7¼ inches
Web site: www.thefancott.co.uk

GENERAL INFORMATION

Nearest Mainline Station: Harlington/Leagrave
Nearest Bus Station: Luton
Car Parking: 50 spaces available on site
Coach Parking: Available but no special space
Souvenir Shop(s): No
Food & Drinks: Pub/Restaurant on site

SPECIAL INFORMATION

The Railway runs through the grounds of The Fancott Pub, winner of the Whitbread Family Pub of the Year in 2000.

OPERATING INFORMATION

Opening Times: Open between Mothers Day and 31st September. 1.00pm to 5.00pm Monday to Thursday, 1.00pm to dusk Friday and Saturday and 12.00pm to dusk on Sundays and Bank Holidays. Only open on weekdays during the School Holidays however.
Steam Working: Steam locos visit on a regular basis – see the website for details.
Prices: £1.00 Adults and Children

Detailed Directions by Car:
From All Parts: Exit the M1 at Junction 12 and travel towards Toddington. After approximately 100 years, take the B579 towards Chalton and Fancott. The Fancott pub is on the left after the second bend.

FFESTINIOG RAILWAY

Address: Ffestiniog Railway, Harbour Station, Porthmadog, Gwynedd LL49 9NF	**Nº of Steam Locos**: 12
Telephone Nº: (01766) 516000	**Nº of Other Locos**: 12
Year Formed: 1832	**Nº of Members**: 5,000
Location of Line: Porthmadog to Blaenau Ffestiniog	**Annual Membership Fee**: £22.00
	Approx Nº of Visitors P.A.: 140,000
Length of Line: 13½ miles	**Gauge**: 1 foot 11½ inches
	Web Site: www.festrail.co.uk

GENERAL INFORMATION

Nearest Mainline Station: Blaenau Ffestiniog (interchange) or Minffordd
Nearest Bus Station: Bus stop next to stations at Porthmadog & Blaenau Ffestiniog
Car Parking: Parking available at Porthmadog, Blaenau Ffestiniog and Minffordd
Coach Parking: Available at Porthmadog and Blaenau Ffestiniog
Souvenir Shop(s): Yes
Food & Drinks: Yes

SPECIAL INFORMATION

The Railway runs through the spectacular scenery of Snowdonia National Park.

OPERATING INFORMATION

Opening Times: Daily service from the 28th March to 5th November. Also a number of other dates during March and November. Limited service in the Winter. Train times vary.
Steam Working: Most trains are steam hauled. Limited in the Winter, however.
Prices: Adult £16.50 (All-day Rover ticket)
Child £8.25 (1 child free with each adult)
Reductions are available for Senior Citizens, Families and groups of 20 or more.

Detailed Directions by Car:
Portmadog is easily accessible from the Midlands – take the M54/A5 to Corwen then the A494 to Bala onto the A4212 to Trawsfynydd and the A470 (becomes the A487 from Maentwrog) to Porthmadog. From Chester take the A55 to Llandudno Junction and the A470 to Blaenau Ffestiniog. Both Stations are well-signposted.

GARTELL LIGHT RAILWAY

Address: Common Lane, Yenston, Templecombe, Somerset   BA8 0NB
Telephone Nº: (01963) 370752
Year Formed: 1991
Location of Line: South of Templecombe
Length of Line: ¾ mile

Nº of Steam Locos: 1
Nº of Other Locos: 3
Approx Nº of Visitors P.A.: 3,000
Gauge: 2 feet
Web site: www.glr-online.co.uk

GENERAL INFORMATION

Nearest Mainline Station: Templecombe (1¼ miles)
Nearest Bus Station: Wincanton
Car Parking: Free parking adjacent to the station
Coach Parking: Adjacent to the station
Souvenir Shop(s): Yes
Food & Drinks: Meals, snacks and drinks available

SPECIAL INFORMATION

The railway is fully signalled using a variety of semaphore, colour-light and shunting signals, controlled by signalmen in two operational signal boxes. Part of the line runs along the track bed of the old Somerset & Dorset Joint Railway.

OPERATING INFORMATION

Opening Times: 17th April; 1st May, 29th May; 25th June; 30th July; 6th, 13th, 20th, 27th & 28th August; 24th September and 29th October. Trains depart at frequent intervals from 10.30am – 4.30pm
Steam Working: Every day the railway is open
Prices: Adult £5.00
　　　　　　 Senior Citizen £4.00
　　　　　　 Child £2.50
Note: Tickets permit unlimited travel by any train on the day of purchase. Under-5s travel for free.

Detailed Directions by Car:
From All Parts: The Railway is situated off the A357 just south of Templecombe and on open days is clearly indicated by the usual brown tourist signs.

GIANT'S CAUSEWAY & BUSHMILLS RAILWAY

Address: Giant's Causeway Station, Runkerry Road, Bushmills, Co. Antrim, Northern Ireland BT57 8SZ **Telephone N°:** (028) 2073-2844 **Information Line:** (028) 2073-2594 **Year Formed:** 2002 **Location:** Between the distillery village of Bushmills and the Giant's Causeway	**Length of Line:** 2 miles **N° of Steam Locos:** 2 **N° of Other Locos:** 1 **N° of Members:** None **Approx N° of Visitors P.A.:** 50,000 **Gauge:** 3 feet **Web site:** www.giantscausewayrailway.org

GENERAL INFORMATION

Nearest Northern Ireland Railway Station: Coleraine/Portrush

Nearest Bus Station: Coleraine/Portrush

Car Parking: Free parking available on site. By parking at the Bushmills Station and taking the railway expensive parking charges at the Causeway itself can be avoided.

Coach Parking: Available on site

Souvenir Shop(s): Yes

Food & Drinks: At Giant's Causeway Station only

SPECIAL INFORMATION

The railway links the distillery village of Bushmills (open to visitors) to the World Heritage Site of the Giant's Causeway. The railway itself is built on the final two miles of the pioneering hydro-electric tramway which linked the Giant's Causeway to the main railway at Portrush from 1883 to 1949.

OPERATING INFORMATION

Opening Times: Usually daily from mid-May to the end of September and for two weeks over Easter. Also open at weekends from Easter until mid-May and during October. Trains run from 11.00am.

Steam Working: Usually daily. Please ring the Information Line shown above for more details.

Prices: Adult Return £5.00
              Adult Single £3.50
              Child Return £3.00
              Child Single £2.00

Note: Family Tickets are also available

Detailed Directions by Car:

From Belfast take the M2 to the junction with the A26 (for Antrim, Ballymena and Coleraine). Follow the A26/M2/A26. From Ballymoney onwards Bushmills and the Giant's Causeway are well signposted. The railway is also well signposted in the immediate vicinity.

GOLDEN VALLEY LIGHT RAILWAY

Address: Butterley Station, Ripley, Derbyshire   DE5 3QZ
Telephone Nº: (01773) 747674
Year Formed: 1987
Location of Line: Butterley, near Ripley
Length of Line: Four-fifths of a mile
Web site: www.gvlr.org.uk

Nº of Steam Locos: 2
Nº of Other Locos: 21
Nº of Members: 75
Annual Membership Fee: £14.00
Approx Nº of Visitors P.A.: 10,000
Gauge: 2 feet

GENERAL INFORMATION

Nearest Mainline Station: Alfreton (6 miles)
Nearest Bus Station: Bus stop outside the Station
Car Parking: Free parking at site – ample space
Coach Parking: Free parking at site
Souvenir Shop(s): Yes – at Butterley and Swanwick
Food & Drinks: Yes – both sites

SPECIAL INFORMATION

The Golden Valley Light Railway is part of the Midland Railway – Butterley and runs from the museum site through the country park to Newlands Inn Station close to the Cromford Canal and the pub of the same name.

OPERATING INFORMATION

Opening Times: Weekends and Bank Holidays from April to October and daily from 14th to 23rd April, 27th May to 4th June and 22nd July to 4th September. Trains run from 12.30pm onwards.
Steam Working: One weekend per month – please contact the railway for further details.
Prices: Adult £1.50
Children 50p

Detailed Directions by Car:
From All Parts: From the M1 exit at Junction 28 and take the A38 towards Derby. The Centre is signposted at the junction with the B6179.

GREAT WHIPSNADE RAILWAY

Address: Whipsnade Wild Animal Park, Dunstable   LU6 2LF
Telephone Nº: (01582) 872171
Year Formed: 1970
Location of Line: Whipsnade Zoo, Near Dunstable
Length of Line: 1¾ miles

Nº of Steam Locos: 2
Nº of Other Locos: 5
Nº of Members: None
Approx Nº of Visitors P.A.: 130,000
Gauge: 2 feet 6 inches
Web site: www.zsl.org

GENERAL INFORMATION

Nearest Mainline Station: Luton (7 miles)
Nearest Bus Station: Dunstable (3 miles)
Car Parking: Available just outside the park
Coach Parking: Available just outside the park
Souvenir Shop(s): Next to the Station
Food & Drinks: Available

SPECIAL INFORMATION

The Railway is situated in the Whipsnade Wild Animal Park.

OPERATING INFORMATION

Opening Times: Daily from 10.00am to 6.00pm throughout the year.
Steam Working: Every operating day.
Prices: Adult Return £2.75
          Child Return £2.25

Detailed Directions by Car:
From All Parts: Exit the M1 at Junction 11 and take the A505 then the B489. Follow signs for Whipsnade Zoo.

GROUDLE GLEN RAILWAY

Address: Groudle Glen, Onchan, Isle of Man	**Nº of Steam Locos:** 2
Telephone Nº: (01624) 670453 (weekends)	**Nº of Other Locos:** 2
Year Formed: 1982 **Re-Opened:** 1986	**Nº of Members:** 600
Location of Line: Groudle Glen	**Annual Membership Fee:** £10.00
Length of Line: ¾ mile	**Approx Nº of Visitors P.A.:** 10,000
Gauge: Narrow	**Correspondence:** 29 Hawarden Avenue, Douglas, Isle of Man IM1 4BP

GENERAL INFORMATION

Nearest Mainline Station: Manx Electric Railway
Nearest Bus Station: Douglas Bus Station
Car Parking: At the entrance to the Glen
Coach Parking: At the entrance to the Glen
Souvenir Shop(s): Yes
Food & Drinks: Coffee and Tea available

SPECIAL INFORMATION

The Railway runs through a picturesque glen to a coastal headland where there are the remains of a Victorian Zoo. The Railway was built in 1896 and closed in 1962.

OPERATING INFORMATION

Opening Times: Easter Sunday & Monday + Sundays from 30th April to 24th September 11.00am to 4.30pm. Also Tuesday evenings from 1st to 22nd August and Wednesday evenings from 5th July to 23rd August. Santa trains run on 17th, 23rd and 24th December + Boxing Day.
Steam Working: Phone the Railway for details.
Prices: Adult Return £3.00
Child Return £1.50
Santa train fares £5.00

Detailed Directions by Car:
The Railway is situated on the coast road to the north of Douglas.

HAYLING SEASIDE RAILWAY

Address: Beachlands, Sea Front Road, Hayling Island, Hampshire PO11 9AG
Telephone Nº: (02392) 372427
Year Formed: 2001
Location: Beachlands to Eastoke Corner
Length of Line: 1 mile

Nº of Steam Locos: None
Nº of Other Locos: 3
Nº of Members: Approximately 100
Annual Membership Fee: £10.00
Approx Nº of Visitors P.A.: 25,000
Gauge: 2 feet
Web site: www.easthaylinglightrailway.co.uk

GENERAL INFORMATION

Nearest Mainline Station: Havant
Nearest Bus Station: Beachlands
Car Parking: Spaces are available at both Beachlands and Eastoke Corner.
Coach Parking: Beachlands and Eastoke Corner
Souvenir Shop(s): Yes
Food & Drinks: Available

SPECIAL INFORMATION

The Railway runs along Hayling Island beach front between Beachlands Station and Eastoke Corner.

OPERATING INFORMATION

Opening Times: Every Saturday, Sunday and Wednesday throughout the year and daily during the School holidays. Various specials run at different times of the year including School Half-term weeks beginning 29th May and 23rd October – please phone for details. The first train normally departs at 11.00am from Beachlands.
Steam Working: None
Prices: Adult Return £2.50
　　　　Child/Senior Citizen Return £1.50
　　　　Family Return £5.00 (2 Adult + 2 Child)

Detailed Directions by Car:
Exit the A27 at Havant Roundabout and proceed to Hayling Island and Beachlands Station following the road signs. Parking is available south of the Carousel Amusement Park. Beachlands Station is within the car park.

HEATHERSLAW LIGHT RAILWAY

Address: Ford Forge, Heatherslaw,
Cornhill-on-Tweed   TD12 4TJ
Telephone Nº: (01890) 820244
Year Formed: 1989
Location of Line: Ford & Etal Estates
between Wooler & Berwick
Length of Line: 2 miles

Nº of Steam Locos: 1
Nº of Other Locos: 1
Nº of Members: None
Approx Nº of Visitors P.A.: 30,000
Gauge: 15 inches
Web site: www.ford-and-etal.co.uk
or   www.secretkingdom.com

GENERAL INFORMATION

Nearest Mainline Station: Berwick-upon-Tweed
(10 miles)
Nearest Bus Station: Berwick-upon-Tweed (10 mls)
Car Parking: Available on site
Coach Parking: Available on site
Souvenir Shop(s): Yes
Food & Drinks: Available

SPECIAL INFORMATION

The Railway follows the River Till from Heatherslaw
to Etal Village. All coaching stock is built on site.

OPERATING INFORMATION

Opening Times: Daily from 3rd April to 29th
October. Trains run hourly from 11.00am to 3.00pm
Steam Working: Daily except when maintenance is
is being carried out on the engine.
Prices: Adult Return £5.50
           Child Return £3.50   (Under 5's: £1.00)
           Senior Citizen Return £4.50

Detailed Directions by Car:
From the North: Take the A697 from Coldstream and the railway is about 5 miles along; From the South: Take
the A697 from Wooler and Millfield.

HILLS MINIATURE RAILWAY

Address: Hills Garden Centre, London Road, Allostock, Knutsford, Cheshire, WA16 9LU
Telephone Nº: (01565) 722567
Year Formed: 2000
Location of Line: Hills Garden Centre

Length of Line: 800 yards
Nº of Steam Locos: 2
Nº of Other Locos: 3
Approx Nº of Visitors P.A.: 12,000
Gauge: 7¼ inches
Web site: www.hills-miniature-railway.co.uk

GENERAL INFORMATION

Nearest Mainline Station: Holmes Chapel (4 miles)
Nearest Bus Station: Holmes Chapel (4 miles)
Car Parking: Spaces for 80 cars on site
Coach Parking: One space available on site
Souvenir Shop(s): Yes
Food & Drinks: Yes

SPECIAL INFORMATION

The Railway runs through the landscaped grounds of the Hills Garden Centre.

OPERATING INFORMATION

Opening Times: The Railway opens on weekends and Bank Holidays throughout the year. Trains run from 11.00am to 4.00pm. All train times are weather permitting.
Steam Working: Daily when operating
Prices: Adult £1.00 per ride
　　　　　Child 50p per ride (Under-2s free)
　　　　　10 ride ticket £8.00

Detailed Directions by Car:
From the North & South: Exit the M6 at Junction 18 and follow the A54 to Holmes Chapel. In Holmes Chapel turn left onto the A50 London Road and follow for 5 miles. Hills Garden Centre is on the left hand side.

HOLLYCOMBE STEAM COLLECTION

Address: Hollycombe, Liphook, Hants. GU30 7LP	**N° of Steam Locos**: 3
Telephone N°: (01428) 724900	**N° of Other Locos**: 1
Year Formed: 1970	**N° of Members**: 100
Location of Line: Hollycombe, Liphook	**Annual Membership Fee**: £8.00
Length of Line: 1¾ miles Narrow gauge, ¼ mile Standard gauge	**Approx N° of Visitors P.A.**: 35,000
	Gauge: 2 feet (narrow gauge)
	Web site: www.hollycombe.co.uk

GENERAL INFORMATION
Nearest Mainline Station: Liphook (1 mile)
Nearest Bus Station: Liphook
Car Parking: Extensive grass area
Coach Parking: Hardstanding
Souvenir Shop(s): Yes
Food & Drinks: Yes – Cafe

SPECIAL INFORMATION
The narrow gauge railway ascends to spectacular views of the Downs and is part of an extensive working steam museum.

OPERATING INFORMATION
Opening Times: Sundays and Bank Holidays from 9th April to 8th October. Open daily from 30th July to 28th August.
Steam Working: 1.00pm to 5.00pm
Prices: Adult £9.00
  Child £7.50
  Family £30.00 (4 people with no more than 2 adults)
Note: Prices are £1.00 less on Summer weekdays

Detailed Directions by Car:
Take the A3 to Liphook and follow the brown tourist signs for the railway.

ISLE OF MAN STEAM RAILWAY

Address: Isle of Man Transport, Banks Circus, Douglas, Isle of Man   IM1 5PT
Telephone Nº: (01624) 663366
Year Formed: 1873
Location of Line: Douglas to Port Erin
Length of Line: 15½ miles

Nº of Steam Locos: 7
Nº of Other Locos: 2
Nº of Members: –
Annual Membership Fee: –
Approx Nº of Visitors P.A.: 140,000
Gauge: 3 feet

GENERAL INFORMATION

Nearest Mainline Station: Not applicable
Car Parking: Limited parking at all stations
Coach Parking: Available at Douglas & Port Erin
Souvenir Shop(s): At Port Erin station
Food & Drinks: Yes – Douglas & Port Erin stations

SPECIAL INFORMATION

The Isle of Man Steam Railway is operated by the Isle of Man Government.

OPERATING INFORMATION

Opening Times: Daily from 21st March to 30th October.
Steam Working: All scheduled services
Prices: Prices vary with 1, 3, 5 & 7 day Explorer tickets also available which include travel on buses, the Snaefell and Manx Electric Railways and Douglas Corporation Horse Trams.

Detailed Directions:
By Sea from Heysham (Lancashire) or Liverpool to reach Isle of Man. By Air from Belfast, Dublin, Glasgow, Liverpool, Manchester, Newcastle, Bristol and London. Douglas Station is ½ mile inland from the Sea terminal at the end of North Quay.

KERR'S MINIATURE RAILWAY

Address: West Links Park, Arbroath, Tayside, Scotland
Telephone N°: (01241) 879249
Year Formed: 1935
Location of Line: Seafront, West Links
Length of Line: 400 yards
Web site: www.geocities.com/kmr_scotland

N° of Steam Locos: 3
N° of Other Locos: 4
N° of Members: None
Annual Membership Fee: –
Approx N° of Visitors P.A.: 17,000
Gauge: 10¼ inches

GENERAL INFORMATION

Nearest Mainline Station: Arbroath (1½ miles)
Nearest Bus Station: Arbroath (1½ miles)
Car Parking: Available 600 yards from railway
Coach Parking: Available 600 yards from railway
Souvenir Shop(s): None
Food & Drinks: Cafe in West Links Park

SPECIAL INFORMATION

The Railway is Scotland's oldest passenger-carrying miniature railway. It is a family-run enterprise not run for profit which is staffed by volunteers. The track itself runs alongside the Dundee to Aberdeen mainline.

OPERATING INFORMATION

Opening Times: Weekends only in April, May, June and September. Daily during July and the first half of August then weekends only for the second half of August. Official opening times are 2.00pm to 5.00pm but trains usually run from noon onwards. Please note operation is weather permitting.
Steam Working: No set pattern but Steam is more likely to be running on Sundays than other dates.
Prices: Adult Return £1.00
Child Return £1.00

Detailed Directions by Car:
From All Parts: West Links Park is a seaside location which runs parallel to the A92 Coastal Tourist Route in Abroath. Turn off the A92 at the Seaforth Hotel for parking. The railway is then 600 yards due West along the seafront.

KIRKLEES LIGHT RAILWAY

Address: Park Mill Way, Clayton West, near Huddersfield, W. Yorks. HD8 9XJ **Telephone N°**: (01484) 865727 **Year Formed**: 1991 **Location of Line**: Clayton West to Shelley **Length of Line**: 4 miles	**N° of Steam Locos**: 4 **N° of Other Locos**: 2 **N° of Members**: – **Approx N° of Visitors P.A.**: – **Gauge**: 15 inches **Web site**: www.kirkleeslightrailway.com

GENERAL INFORMATION

Nearest Mainline Station: Denby Dale (4 miles)
Nearest Bus Station: Bus stop outside gates. Take 484 from Wakefield or 235 from Huddersfield/Barnsley.
Car Parking: Ample free parking at site
Coach Parking: Ample free parking at site
Souvenir Shop(s): Yes
Food & Drinks: Yes

SPECIAL INFORMATION

The Railway is under new ownership from January 2006 and a new indoor/outdoor play area and cafe is planned for later in the year.

OPERATING INFORMATION

Opening Times: Open every weekend (except 25/26 December) and most school holidays in the Winter. Open daily from 27th May to 3rd September.
Steam Working: All trains are steam-hauled. Trains run hourly from 11.00am
Prices: Adults £6.00
　　　　　Children (3-15 years) £4.00
　　　　　Children (under 3 years) Free of charge
　　　　　Family Ticket £18.00

Detailed Directions by Car:
The Railway is located on the A636 Wakefield to Denby Dale road. Turn off the M1 at Junction 38 and the railway is 4 miles on the left after going under the railway bridge, just before the village of Scissett.

KNEBWORTH PARK MINIATURE RAILWAY

Address: c/o Estate Office, Knebworth, Hertfordshire SG3 6PY
Telephone Nº: (01438) 812661
Year Formed: 1991 (Miniature Railway)
Location of Line: Knebworth Park
Length of Line: 800 yards

Nº of Steam Locos: None
Nº of Other Locos: 7
Nº of Members: None
Approx Nº of Visitors P.A.: 44,000
Gauge: 10¼ inches
Web site: None

GENERAL INFORMATION

Nearest Mainline Station: Knebworth
Nearest Bus Station: Stevenage
Car Parking: Available on site
Coach Parking: Available on site
Souvenir Shop(s): Yes
Food & Drinks: Yes

SPECIAL INFORMATION

The Railway is located in the grounds of the historic Knebworth House.

OPERATING INFORMATION

Opening Times: Daily from 1st to 17th April, 27th May to 4th June and 1st July to 4th September. Weekends and Bank Holidays only from 22nd April to 21st May, 10th to 25th June and 9th to 24th September. Trains run from 11.00am to 5.30pm
Steam Working: None
Prices: Adult £7.00 – £9.00
Child £7.00 – £8.50
Note: Prices shown above are for entrance into Knebworth Park and House. One free train ride is included with the entrance fee. Subsequent rides are charged as follows: Adult £1.50 Child £1.20

Detailed Directions by Car:
From All Parts: Exit the A1(M) at Junction 7 and follow signs for Knebworth Park. After entering the Park, follow signs for the Adventure Playground for the Railway.

LAPPA VALLEY STEAM RAILWAY

Address: St. Newlyn East, Newquay, Cornwall TR8 5HZ	**N° of Steam Locos:** 2
Telephone N°: (01872) 510317	**N° of Other Locos:** 2
Year Formed: 1974	**N° of Members:** –
Location of Line: Benny Halt to East Wheal Rose, near St. Newlyn East	**Annual Membership Fee:** –
Length of Line: 1 mile	**Approx N° of Visitors P.A.:** 50,000
	Gauge: 15 inches
	Web site: www.lappavalley.co.uk

GENERAL INFORMATION

Nearest Mainline Station: Newquay (5 miles)
Nearest Bus Station: Newquay (5 miles)
Car Parking: Free parking at Benny Halt
Coach Parking: Free parking at Benny Halt
Souvenir Shop(s): Yes
Food & Drinks: Yes

SPECIAL INFORMATION

The railway runs on part of the former Newquay to Chacewater branch line. Site also has a Grade II listed mine building, boating, play areas for children and 2 other miniature train rides.

OPERATING INFORMATION

Opening Times: Easter to late October (daily to early October). Limited opening during April and October – please phone the Railway for further details.
Steam Working: 10.30am to 4.30pm or later on operating days
Prices: Adult £7.00
Child £5.50
Senior Citizens £6.00
Family £22.50
(2 adults + 2 children)

Detailed Directions by Car:
The railway is signposted from the A30 at the Summercourt-Mitchell bypass, from the A3075 south of Newquay and the A3058 east of Newquay.

LAUNCESTON STEAM RAILWAY

Address: The Old Gasworks, St. Thomas' Road, Launceston, Cornwall PL15 8DA	**Nº of Steam Locos:** 5 (3 working)
Telephone Nº: (01566) 775665	**Nº of Other Locos:** 2 Diesel, 2 Electric
Year Formed: Opened in 1983	**Nº of Members:** Not applicable
Location of Line: Launceston to Newmills	**Annual Membership Fee:** –
Length of Line: 2½ miles	**Gauge:** 1 foot 11 ⅝ inches
	Web site: www.launcestonsr.co.uk

GENERAL INFORMATION

Nearest Mainline Station: Liskeard (15 miles)
Nearest Bus Station: Launceston (½ mile) – Devon Bus services stop at the Railway on Sundays only
Car Parking: At Station, Newport Industrial Estate, Launceston
Coach Parking: As above
Souvenir Shop(s): Yes – also with a bookshop
Food & Drinks: Yes – Cafe, snacks & drinks

SPECIAL INFORMATION

During the Summer school holidays, two engines are sometimes in operation.

OPERATING INFORMATION

Opening Times: Daily from 28th May until the 15th September but closed on Saturdays.
Steam Working: 11.00am to 4.50pm.
Prices: Adult £6.80
Child £4.50
Family £21.00 (2 adults + 4 children)
Senior Citizen £5.50
Group rates are available upon application. These prices include as many trips as you like on the day of purchase.

Detailed Directions by Car:
From the East/West: Drive to Launceston via the A30 and look for the brown Steam Engine Tourist signs. Use the L.S.R. car park at the Newport Industrial Estate; From Bude/Holsworthy: Take the A388 to Launceston and follow signs for the town centre. After the river bridge turn left at the traffic lights into Newport Industrial Estate and use the L.S.R. car park.

LEADHILLS & WANLOCKHEAD RAILWAY

Address: The Station, Leadhills,
Lanarkshire   ML12 6XS
Telephone Nº: None
Year Formed: 1983
Location of Line: Leadhills, Lanarkshire
Length of Line: ¾ mile (at present)

Nº of Steam Locos: None at present
Nº of Other Locos: 4
Nº of Members: Approximately 100
Annual Membership Fee: Adult £8.00
Approx Nº of Visitors P.A.: 2,500
Gauge: 2 feet
Web site: www.leadhillsrailway.co.uk

GENERAL INFORMATION

Nearest Mainline Station: Sanquhar
Nearest Bus Station: Lanark and Sanquhar
Car Parking: Available on site
Coach Parking: Available on site
Souvenir Shop(s): Yes
Food & Drinks: Yes

SPECIAL INFORMATION

Leadhills & Wanlockhead Railway is the highest
adhesion railway in the UK with the summit 1,498
feet above sea level.

OPERATING INFORMATION

Opening Times: Weekends and Bank Holidays
from Easter until the end of October (Sundays only
in October). Trains run from 11.20am to 4.20pm
Steam Working: None at present
Prices: Adult Day Ticket £3.00
Child Day Ticket £1.00
Family Day Ticket £7.00
Senior Citizen Day Ticket £2.50

Detailed Directions by Car:
From the South: Exit the M74 at Junction 14 and follow the A702 to Elvanfoot. Turn right onto the B7040 and
follow to Leadhills. Turn left at the T-junction and Station Road is a short distance on the left; From the North: Exit
the M74 at Junction 13 for Abington and follow signs for Leadhills along the B797. Station Road is on the left
shortly after entering Leadhills.

LEIGHTON BUZZARD RAILWAY

Address: Pages Park Station, Billington Road, Leighton Buzzard, Beds. LU7 4TN	**Nº of Steam Locos**: 12
Telephone Nº: (01525) 373888	**Nº of Other Locos**: 41
Year Formed: 1967	**Nº of Members**: 400
Location of Line: Leighton Buzzard	**Annual Membership Fee**: £16.00
Length of Line: 3 miles	**Approx Nº of Visitors P.A.**: 21,000
	Gauge: 2 feet

GENERAL INFORMATION

Nearest Mainline Station: Leighton Buzzard (2 miles)
Nearest Bus Station: Leighton Buzzard (¾ mile)
Car Parking: Free parking adjacent
Coach Parking: Free parking adjacent
Souvenir Shop(s): Yes
Food & Drinks: Yes

Web site: www.buzzrail.co.uk

OPERATING INFORMATION

Opening Times: Sundays from 13th March to 30th October plus Bank Holiday weekends. Also open on some Saturdays and weekdays. Trains run from mid-morning to late afternoon and Santa Specials run on some dates in December. Contact the railway further details.
Steam Working: Most operating days.
Prices: Adult £6.00
Child £3.00
Senior Citizens £5.00
Family Ticket £17.00 (2 Adult + 2 Child)

Detailed Directions by Car:
The railway is 15 minutes drive from Junctions 11-13 of the M1. Follow the brown tourist signs in Leighton Buzzard or from the A505. Pages Park Station is ¾ mile from the Town Centre on the A4146 Hemel Hempstead road.

LIONS MANE LINE MINIATURE RAILWAY

Address: Saville Bros Garden Centre, Selby Road, Garforth, Leeds LS25 2AQ	**Nº of Steam Locos**: None
Telephone Nº: (0113) 286-2183	**Nº of Other Locos**: 1
Year Formed: 1978	**Nº of Members**: –
Location of Line: A63 Garforth to Selby	**Approx Nº of Visitors P.A.**: 10,500
Length of Line: ½ mile	**Gauge**: 10¼ inches
	Web site: www.garforthlions.ik.com

GENERAL INFORMATION

Nearest Mainline Station: Garforth
Nearest Bus Station: Garforth
Car Parking: Available on site
Coach Parking: Available on site
Souvenir Shop(s): No
Food & Drinks: Café on site

SPECIAL INFORMATION

The Rio Grande Train, owned by William Strike Ltd., is operated by volunteers from Garforth & District Lions Club with the profits going to support a variety of needy causes.

OPERATING INFORMATION

Opening Times: Weekends and Bank Holidays from March to September. Trains run from 11.00am to 4.00pm.
Steam Working: None
Prices: Adult Return £1.00
                   Child Return £1.00

Detailed Directions by Car:
From the M1 and M62: Take the A1(M) north and exit at Junction 46. Follow the A63 towards Selby and go straight on at the next roundabout with the Old George Pub on the left. Continue straight on up the hill passing the Crusader pub on the left and the Garden Centre is on the left; From the A1: Exit the A1 onto the A63 (Milford Lodge Hotel) and follow signs towards Leeds. Go straight on at the first roundabout and the Garden Centre is on the right after approximately ½ mile.

LLANBERIS LAKE RAILWAY

Address: Gilfach Ddu, Llanberis,
Gwynedd   LL55 4TY
Telephone Nº: (01286) 870549
Year Formed: 1970
Location of Line: Just off the A4086
Caernarfon to Capel Curig road at Llanberis
Length of Line: 2½ miles

Nº of Steam Locos: 3
Nº of Other Locos: 4
Nº of Members: –
Annual Membership Fee: –
Approx Nº of Visitors P.A.: 70,000
Gauge: 1 foot 11½ inches
Web site: www.lake-railway.co.uk

GENERAL INFORMATION

Nearest Mainline Station: Bangor (8 miles)
Nearest Bus Station: Caernarfon (6 miles)
Car Parking: £2.00 Council car park on site
Coach Parking: Ample free parking on site
Souvenir Shop(s): Yes
Food & Drinks: Yes

SPECIAL INFORMATION

Llanberis Lake Railway runs along part of the
trackbed of the Padarn Railway which transported
slates for export and closed in 1961. An extension to
Llanberis village opened in June 2003.

OPERATING INFORMATION

Opening Times: Open most days from mid-March
to 31st October. Please send for a free timetable.
Steam Working: 11.00am to 4.00pm on most days.
Prices: Adult £6.00
            Child £4.00
Various Family ticket options are available.
N.B. The Welsh Slate Museum is adjacent to the
Railway.

Detailed Directions by Car:
The railway is situated just off the A4086 Caernarfon to Capel Curig road. Follow signs for Padarn Country Park.

LYNTON & BARNSTAPLE RAILWAY

Address: Woody Bay Station, Martinhoe Cross, Parracombe, Devon EX31 4RA	**N° of Steam Locos**: 2
Telephone N°: (01598) 763487	**N° of Other Locos**: 2
Year Formed: 1979	**N° of Members**: 1,400
Location of Line: North Devon	**Annual Membership Fee**: £15.00
Length of Line: One mile	**Approx N° of Visitors P.A.**: 25,000
	Gauge: 1 foot 11½ inches
	Web site: www.lynton-rail.co.uk

GENERAL INFORMATION

Nearest Mainline Station: Barnstaple
Nearest Bus Station: Barnstaple
Car Parking: Available at Woody Bay Station
Coach Parking: Available by prior arrangement
Souvenir Shop(s): Yes – at Woody Bay Station
Food & Drinks: Available at Woody Bay Station

SPECIAL INFORMATION

Passengers were first carried on a short stretch of this scenic narrow-gauge railway in July 2004. This was the first time the track had been used since the original railway closed in September 1935. The ultimate aim of the Lynton & Barnstaple Railway Trust is to re-open all 19 miles of the line.

OPERATING INFORMATION

Opening Times: Open most days from Easter until the end of October. Please check with the railway for exact dates before visting. Also open for Santa trains in December. Trains run from 11.00am to 4.00pm.
Steam Working: Daily in July and August and on a variety of other dates – phone for details.
Prices: Adult Return £2.50
Child Return £1.50 (Under-14s)
Senior Citizen Return £1.75
Family Ticket £6.00 (2 Adult + 3 Children)

Detailed Directions by Car:
From All Parts: Woody Bay Station is located alongside the A39 halfway between Lynton and Blackmoor Gate and one mile north-east of the village of Parracombe.

MOORS VALLEY RAILWAY

Address: Moors Valley Country Park, Horton Road, Ashley Heath, Nr. Ringwood, Hants. BH24 2ET **Telephone Nº**: (01425) 471415 **Year Formed**: 1985 **Location of Line**: Moors Valley Country Park	**Length of Line**: 1 mile **Nº of Steam Locos**: 15 **Nº of Other Locos**: 2 **Nº of Members**: – **Approx Nº of Visitors P.A.**: – **Gauge**: 7¼ inches **Web site**: www.moorsvalleyrailway.co.uk

GENERAL INFORMATION

Nearest Mainline Station: Bournemouth (12 miles)
Nearest Bus Station: Ringwood (3 miles)
Car Parking: Parking charge varies throughout the year. Maximum charge £5.00 per day.
Coach Parking: Charges are applied for parking
Souvenir Shop(s): Yes + Model Railway Shop
Food & Drinks: Yes

SPECIAL INFORMATION

The Moors Valley Railway is a complete small Railway with signalling and 2 signal boxes and also 4 tunnels and 2 level crossings.

OPERATING INFORMATION

Opening Times: Weekends throughout the year. Daily from one week before to one week after Easter, Spring Bank Holiday to mid-September, during School half-term holidays and also from Boxing Day to end of School holidays. Also Santa Specials in December and occasional other openings. Phone the Railways for details.
Steam Working: 10.45am to 5.00pm when open.
Prices: Adult Return £2.40; Adult Single £1.45
          Child Return £1.80;   Child Single £1.00
Special rates are available for parties of 10 or more.

Detailed Directions by Car:
From All Parts: Moors Valley Country Park is situated on Horton Road which is off the A31 Ferndown to Ringwood road near the junction with the A338 to Bournemouth.

MULL & WEST HIGHLAND RAILWAY

Address: Old Pier Station, Craignure, Isle of Mull, Argyll PA65 6AY **Telephone N°**: (01680) 812494 **Web site**: www.mullrail.co.uk **Year Formed**: 1983 **Location of Line**: Isle of Mull **Length of Line**: 1¼ miles	**Gauge**: 10¼ inches **N° of Steam Locos**: 2 **N° of Other Locos**: 3 **N° of Members**: 30 **Annual Membership Fee**: £5.00 **Approx N° of Visitors P.A.**: 30,000 **Web site**: www.mullrail.co.uk

GENERAL INFORMATION

Nearest Mainline Station: Oban (11 miles by Cal-Mac Ferry)
Nearest Bus Station: Oban (as above)
Car Parking: Free parking on site at Craignure
Coach Parking: Free parking at site
Souvenir Shop(s): Yes
Food & Drinks: No – but drinks & sweets available

SPECIAL INFORMATION

This narrow gauge railway was the first passenger railway to be built on a Scottish island. It was built specially to link Torosay Castle & Gardens to the main Port of entry at Craignure.

OPERATING INFORMATION

Opening Times: Daily from 1st April to 28th October. Opens 11.00am to 5.00pm.
Steam Working: Steam and diesel trains are run depending on operational requirements.
Prices: Adult Single £3.00; Adult Return £4.00
Family Tickets (2 adults + 2 children)
Single £8.50; Return £12.00
Note: Joint Ferry, Train & Castle tickets are available for purchase in Oban. Other special rates are available for Children.

Detailed Directions by Car:
Once off the ferry, turn left at the end of the pier, go straight on for almost ½ mile then turn left at the thistle sign opposite the Police station and carry straight on until you reach the station car park.

NORTH BAY MINIATURE RAILWAY

Address: Peasholme Park Station, Northstead Manor Gardens, Scarborough, North Yorkshire
Year Opened: 1931
Location: Peasholme Park to Scalby Mills
Length of Line: 1 mile

N⁰ of Steam Locos: None
N⁰ of Other Locos: 2
N⁰ of Members: None – Council owned
Approx N⁰ of Visitors P.A.: 76,500
Gauge: 20 inches

GENERAL INFORMATION

Nearest Mainline Station: Scarborough
Nearest Bus Station: Scarborough
Car Parking: Available on site
Coach Parking: Available on site
Souvenir Shop(s): None
Food & Drinks: None

SPECIAL INFORMATION

The North Bay Miniature Railway was opened in 1931 and operates between Northstead Manor and Scalby Mills Sea Life Centre.

OPERATING INFORMATION

Opening Times: Daily from Easter until the end of October. Trains run at varying times, depending on the time of the year.
Steam Working: None
Prices: Adult Return £2.55
Child Return £2.10

Detailed Directions by Car:
From All Parts: Take the A64, A165 or A170 to Scarborough and follow the signs for North Bay. The railway is situated just off the A165 opposite Peasholme Park.

NORTH GLOUCESTERSHIRE RAILWAY

Address: The Station, Toddington, Cheltenham, Gloucestershire   GL54 5DT
Telephone Nº: (01242) 621405
Year Formed: 1985
Location of Line: 5 miles south of Broadway, Worcestershire, near the A46
Length of Line: ½ mile

Nº of Steam Locos: 4
Nº of Other Locos: 5
Nº of Members: –
Annual Membership Fee: –
Approx Nº of Visitors P.A.: –
Gauge: 2 feet
Web site: www.isibutu.pwp.blueyonder.co.uk

GENERAL INFORMATION

Nearest Mainline Station: Cheltenham Spa or Ashchurch
Nearest Bus Station: Cheltenham
Car Parking: Parking available at Toddington, Winchcombe & Cheltenham Racecourse Stations
Coach Parking: Parking available as above
Souvenir Shop(s): Yes
Food & Drinks: Available

SPECIAL INFORMATION

The railway boasts the only German-built World War One Henschel locomotive in this country.

OPERATING INFORMATION

Opening Times: Sundays and Bank Holidays from Easter until the end of August. Also open on 30th September and 1st October. Trains usually run from every 35 minutes from around noon.
Steam Working: Most operating days
Prices: Please contact the railway for details.

Detailed Directions by Car:
Toddington is 11 miles north east of Cheltenham, 5 miles south of Broadway just off the B4632 (old A46). Exit the M5 at Junction 9 towards Stow-on-the-Wold for the B4632. The Railway is clearly visible from the B4632.

NORTH SCARLE MINIATURE RAILWAY

Address: North Scarle Playing Field, Swinderby Road, North Scarle, Lincolnshire
Telephone Nº: (01522) 888228
Year Formed: 1933
Location of Line: North Scarle, between Newark and Lincoln
Length of Line: A third of a mile

Nº of Steam Locos: 7
Nº of Other Locos: 5
Nº of Members: 40
Annual Membership Fee: £25.00
Approx Nº of Visitors P.A.: 3,000
Gauges: 7¼ inches and 5 inches
Web site: www.lincolnmes.co.uk

GENERAL INFORMATION

Nearest Mainline Station: Newark Northgate (5 miles)
Nearest Bus Station: Newark (5 miles)
Car Parking: 300 spaces available on site
Coach Parking: None available
Souvenir Shop(s): None
Food & Drinks: Available on special days only

SPECIAL INFORMATION

The Railway is owned and operated by the Lincoln and District Model Engineering Society which was founded in 1933.

OPERATING INFORMATION

Opening Times: Car Boot Sale Sundays only!
Dates for 2006: 26th March; 9th & 23rd April; 7th & 21st May; 4th & 18th June; 2nd, 16th & 30th July; 13th & 27th August; 10th, 16th, 17th (Special Open Weekend) & 24th September; 8th October.
Steam Working: Every running day.
Prices: Adult Return 50p
Child Return 50p

Detailed Directions by Car:
North Scarle is situated off the A46 between Lincoln and Newark (about 5 miles from Newark). Alternatively, take the A1133 from Gainsborough and follow the North Scarle signs when around 6 miles from Newark.

OLD KILN LIGHT RAILWAY

Address: Rural Life Centre, Reeds Road, Tilford, Farnham, Surrey GU10 2DL
Telephone Nº: (01252) 795571
Year Formed: 1975
Location: 3 miles south of Farnham
Length of Line: A third of a mile
Web site: www.rural-life.org.uk

Nº of Steam Locos: 2
Nº of Other Locos: 10
Nº of Members: 14
Annual Membership Fee: £25.00
Approx Nº of Visitors P.A.: 21,000
Gauge: 2 feet

GENERAL INFORMATION

Nearest Mainline Station: Farnham (4 miles)
Nearest Bus Station: Farnham
Car Parking: Free parking available on site
Coach Parking: Free parking available on site
Souvenir Shop(s): Yes
Food & Drinks: Available

SPECIAL INFORMATION

The Railway is part of the Rural Life Centre at Tilford. The Centre contains the biggest country life collection in the South of England with a wide range of attractions.

OPERATING INFORMATION

Opening Times: The Rural Life Centre is open Wednesday to Sunday and Bank Holidays from 15th March to 8th October 10.00am – 5.00pm. Open Wednesdays and Sundays only during the winter 11.00am – 4.00pm.
Steam Working: Bank Holidays and special events once a month – contact the Centre for details. Diesel at all other times.
Prices: Adult £1.00
    Children £1.00 (Under-5s travel free)

Detailed Directions by Car:
The Rural Life Centre is situated 3 miles south of Farnham. From Farnham take the A287 southwards before turning left at Millbridge crossroads into Reeds Road. The Centre is on the left after about ½ mile, just after the Frensham Garden Centre; From the A3: Turn off at the Hindhead crossroads and head north to Tilford. Pass through Tilford, cross the River Wey then turn left into Reeds Road. The Centre is on the right after ½ mile.

PERRYGROVE RAILWAY

Address: Perrygrove Railway, Coleford, Gloucestershire GL16 8QB	**Nº of Steam Locos**: 3
Telephone Nº: (01594) 834991	**Nº of Other Locos**: 2
Year Formed: 1996	**Nº of Members**: None
Location of Line: ½ mile south of Coleford	**Approx Nº of Visitors P.A.**: Not known
Length of Line: ¾ mile	**Gauge**: 15 inches
	Web site: www.perrygrove.co.uk

GENERAL INFORMATION

Nearest Mainline Station: Lyndney
Nearest Bus Station: Bus stops in Coleford
Car Parking: Free parking available
Coach Parking: Available on site
Souvenir Shop(s): Yes
Food & Drinks: Sandwiches & light refreshments

SPECIAL INFORMATION

Perrygrove is a unique railway with 4 stations, all with access to private woodland walks. Lots of picnic tables are available in the open and under cover. There is also an indoor village with secret passages.

OPERATING INFORMATION

Opening Times: Mondays, Wednesdays, Thursdays and Weekends during most school holidays. Also Thursdays in June and July and many other weekends. Santa Specials at Christmas (pre-bookings are essential). Phone for details. Railway opens at 11.00am with the last train at 4.15pm.
Steam Working: Most services are steam-hauled.
Prices: Adult £4.00 (All-day ticket)
Senior Citizen £3.50 (All-day ticket)
Child (ages 3-16) £3.00 (All-day ticket)

Detailed Directions by Car:
From All Parts: Travel to Coleford, Gloucestershire. Upon reaching the vicinity of Coleford, the Perrygrove Railway is clearly signposted with brown tourist signs from all directions.

PINEWOOD MINIATURE RAILWAY

Address: Pinewood Leisure Centre, Old Wokingham Road, Wokingham, Berkshire RG40 3AQ	**Nº of Steam Locos:** 50 (All owned
	Nº of Other Locos: 30 by Members)
	Nº of Members: Approximately 50
Phone Nº: (01252) 510340 (Secretary)	**Annual Membership Fee:** £35.00
Year Formed: 1984	**Approx Nº of Visitors P.A.:** 2,500
Location: Pinewood Leisure Centre	**Gauge:** 5 inches and 7¼ inches
Length of Line: 700 metres	**Web site:** www.pinewoodrailway.co.uk

GENERAL INFORMATION

Nearest Mainline Station: Bracknell
Nearest Bus Station: Bracknell
Car Parking: Available on site
Coach Parking: Available by arrangement
Souvenir Shop(s): None
Food & Drinks: Tea/Coffee making facilities only

SPECIAL INFORMATION

The Pinewood Miniature Railway runs through attractive woodlands backing on to a Leisure Centre.

OPERATING INFORMATION

Opening Times: Year-round work sessions on Sunday mornings and all day on Wednesdays.
Steam Working: Members Steam Up on 1st Sunday of the month. Public running on the 3rd Sunday in the month from April to October (November if the weather is fine). Santa Specials on some dates in December (pre-booking is advised). Private Parties can sometimes be catered for by prior arrangement.
Prices: 70p per ride

Detailed Directions by Car:
From the M3 or the A30 take the A322 towards Bracknell. Once on the A322, keep in the left hand lane to the first major roundabout then take the first exit onto the B3430 towards Wokingham along Nine Mile Ride. Cross the next roundabout (A3095) and continue on the B3430 passing the Golden Retriever pub and the Crematorium. Go straight on at the next mini-roundabout then turn right at the following roundabout into Old Wokingham Road. The Pinewood Leisure Centre is on the left after approximately 100 metres.

RAVENGLASS & ESKDALE RAILWAY

Address: Ravenglass, Cumbria
CA18 1SW
Telephone Nº: (01229) 717171
Year Formed: 1875
Location: The Lake District National Park
Length of Line: 7 miles

Gauge: 15 inches
Nº of Steam Locos: 6
Nº of Other Locos: 8
Nº of Members: None
Approx Nº of Visitors P.A.: 120,000
Web site: www.ravenglass-railway.co.uk

GENERAL INFORMATION

Nearest Mainline Station: Ravenglass (adjacent)
Nearest Bus Stop: Ravenglass
Car Parking: Available at both terminals
Coach Parking: At Ravenglass
Souvenir Shop(s): Yes
Food & Drinks: Yes

SPECIAL INFORMATION

From Ravenglass, the Lake District's only coastal village, the line runs through two lovely valleys to the foot of England's highest mountain. A brand new Station, Café Restaurant, Gift Shop and Meeting Room is now open at Dalegarth (Eskdale).

OPERATING INFORMATION

Opening Times: The service runs daily from the end of March until the beginning of November. Also runs during most weekends in the Winter, Christmas and February half-term. Open from 9.00am to 5.00pm (sometimes later during high season).
Steam Working: Most services are steam hauled.
Prices: Adult £9.00
Child £4.50

Detailed Directions by Car:
The railway is situated just off the main A595 Western Lake District road.

RHYL MINIATURE RAILWAY

Address: Marine Lake, Wellington Road, Rhyl	**Nº of Steam Locos**: 2
	Nº of Other Locos: 3
Telephone Nº: (01352) 759109	**Nº of Members**: Approximately 50
Year Formed: 1911	**Annual Membership Fee**: £7.50
Location of Line: Rhyl	**Approx Nº of Visitors P.A.**: 5,500
Length of Line: 1 mile	**Gauge**: 15 inches
	Web site: www.rhylminiaturerailway.co.uk

Photo courtesy of John Myers

GENERAL INFORMATION

Nearest Mainline Station: Rhyl (1 mile)
Nearest Bus Station: Rhyl (1 mile)
Car Parking: Car Park opposite the Railway
Coach Parking: Available nearby
Souvenir Shop(s): No
Food & Drinks: Available nearby

SPECIAL INFORMATION

The trust runs the oldest Miniature Railway in the UK. The principal locomotive and train have been operating there since the 1920's.

OPERATING INFORMATION

Opening Times: Bank holiday Sundays and Mondays; every Sunday from 11th June to 10th September; every Thursday and Saturday in the School Summer Holidays. Trains run from 1.00pm to 5.00pm.
Steam Working: All above dates, weather permitting.
Prices: Adult £1.00
Child £1.00

Detailed Directions by Car:
From All Parts: The Railway is located behind the Ocean Beach Funfair at the west end of Rhyl Promenade.

ROMNEY, HYTHE & DYMCHURCH RAILWAY

Address: New Romney Station, New Romney, Kent TN28 8PL	**Nº of Steam Locos**: 11
Telephone Nº: (01797) 362353	**Nº of Other Locos**: 5
Year Formed: 1927	**Nº of Members**: 2,500
Location of Line: Approximately 4 miles south of Folkestone	**Annual Membership Fee**: Supporters association – Adult £16.00; Junior £8.00
Length of Line: 13½ miles	**Approx Nº of Visitors P.A.**: 160,000
	Gauge: 15 inches

GENERAL INFORMATION

Nearest Mainline Station: Folkestone Central (4 miles)
Nearest Bus Station: Folkestone (then take bus to Hythe)
Car Parking: Available at all major stations
Coach Parking: At New Romney & Dungeness
Souvenir Shop(s): Yes – 4 at various stations
Food & Drinks: 2 Cafes serving food and drinks

SPECIAL INFORMATION

Opened in 1927 as 'The World's Smallest Public Railway'. Now the only 15" gauge tourist main line railway in the world. Double track, 6 stations.

OPERATING INFORMATION

Opening Times: A daily service runs from 1st April to 30th September. Open at weekends in February, March and October and for Santa Specials in December. Open daily during School half-terms.
Steam Working: All operational days.
Prices: Depends on length of journey. Maximums:
Adult £10.90
Child £5.45
Family £30.50 (2 adult + 2 children)

Web Site: www.rhdr.org.uk

Detailed Directions by Car:
Exit the M20 at Junction 11 then follow signs to Hythe and the brown tourist signs for the railway. Alternatively, Take the A259 to New Romney and follow the brown tourist signs for the railway.

ROYAL VICTORIA RAILWAY

Address: Royal Victoria Country Park, Netley, Southampton SO31 5GA **Telephone Nº:** (023) 8045-6246 **Year Formed:** 1995 **Location of Line:** Netley **Length of Line:** 1 mile	**Nº of Steam Locos:** 10 **Nº of Other Locos:** 9 **Nº of Members:** None **Approx Nº of Visitors P.A.:** Not known **Gauge:** 10¼ inches **Web site:** www.royalvictoriarailway.co.uk

Photo courtesy of H. Allenby

GENERAL INFORMATION

Nearest Mainline Station: Netley
Nearest Bus Station: Southampton
Car Parking: Available on site – £1.20 fee
Coach Parking: Free parking available on site
Souvenir Shop(s): Yes
Food & Drinks: Yes

SPECIAL INFORMATION

The railway runs through the grounds of an old Victorian hospital and has good views of the Solent and the Isle of Wight. The Park covers 200 acres includingwoodland, grassland, beaches and picnic sites.

OPERATING INFORMATION

Opening Times: Weekends throughout the year and daily during school holidays. Also by appointment for larger parties.
Steam Working: Saturdays and all specials. Please phone for further details.
Prices: Adult Return £1.50
Child Return £1.00
Note: Special rates are available for groups of 10 or more when pre-booked. Under-2s travel free.

Detailed Directions by Car:
From All Parts: Exit the M27 at Junction 8 and follow the Brown Tourist signs for the Royal Victoria Country Park. You will reach the Park after approximately 3 miles.

RUDYARD LAKE STEAM RAILWAY

Address: Rudyard Station, Rudyard, Near Leek, Staffordshire ST13 8PF **Telephone N°**: (01995) 672280 **Year Formed**: 1985 **Location**: Rudyard to Hunthouse Wood **Length of Line**: 1½ miles	**N° of Steam Locos**: 5 **N° of Other Locos**: 2 **N° of Members**: – **Approx N° of Visitors P.A.**: 27,500 **Gauge**: 10¼ inches **Web site**: www.rudyardlakerailway.co.uk

GENERAL INFORMATION

Nearest Mainline Station: Stoke-on-Trent (10 miles)
Nearest Bus Station: Leek
Car Parking: Free parking at Rudyard Station
Coach Parking: Free parking at Rudyard Station
Souvenir Shop(s): Yes
Food & Drinks: Yes – Cafe at Dam Station

SPECIAL INFORMATION

The Railway runs along the side of the historic Rudyard Lake that gave author Rudyard Kipling his name. A Steamboat also plies the lake at times. "Drive a Steam Train" courses can be booked.

OPERATING INFORMATION

Opening Times: Every Sunday and Bank Holiday from mid-March to the end of October. Also open on every Saturday from 1st May to 30th September and every Tuesday, Wednesday and Thursday from 25th July to 31st August. Santa Specials also run on 10th and 17th December.
Steam Working: All trains are normally steam hauled. Trains run from 11.00am on Sundays, Bank Holidays and during Midweek and from 1.00pm on Saturdays. The last train runs around 4.00pm.
Prices: Adult Return £3.00
Child Return £2.00
A variety of other fares are also available.

Detailed Directions by Car:
From All Parts: Head for Leek then follow the A523 North towards Macclesfield for 1 mile. Follow the brown tourist signs to the B5331 signposted for Rudyard for ½ mile. Pass under the Railway bridge and turn immediately left and go up the ramp to the Station car park.

RUISLIP LIDO RAILWAY

Address: Reservoir Road, Ruislip, Middlesex HA4 7TY
Telephone Nº: (01895) 622595
Year Formed: 1979
Location of Line: Trains travel from Ruislip Lido to Woody Bay
Length of Line: 1¼ miles

Nº of Steam Locos: 1
Nº of Other Locos: 5
Nº of Members: 155
Annual Membership Fee: £15.00
Approx Nº of Visitors P.A.: 60,000
Gauge: 12 inches
Web site: www.ruisliplidorailway.org

Photo courtesy of Peter Musgrave

GENERAL INFORMATION

Nearest Mainline Station: West Ruislip (2 miles)
Nearest Bus Station: Ruislip Underground Station
Car Parking: Free parking available at the Lido
Coach Parking: Free parking available at the Lido
Souvenir Shop(s): Yes
Food & Drinks: A Beach Cafe is open on Sundays and Bank Holidays. A Pub/Restaurant is open daily.

SPECIAL INFORMATION

The steam locomotive, 'Mad Bess' used by Ruislip Lido Railway was actually built by the members over a 12 year period!

OPERATING INFORMATION

Opening Times: Weekends from mid-February to the end of May and also daily during school holidays. Also open on weekends from September to November and on Sundays in December.
Steam Working: Sundays and Bank Holidays from July to the end of September and also Santa Specials.
Prices: Adult Return £1.70 (Single fare £1.40)
Child Return £1.30 (Single fare £1.10)
Family Return £5.00 (Single fare £4.00)
(2 adults + 2 children)

Detailed Directions by Car:
From All Parts: Follow the signs from the A40 and take the A4180 through Ruislip before turning left onto the B469.

SITTINGBOURNE & KEMSLEY LIGHT RAILWAY

Address: P.O. Box 300, Sittingbourne, Kent ME10 2DZ	**N⁰ of Steam Locos:** 9 (2 Standard gauge)
Advance Bookings: (0871) 222-1569	**N⁰ of Other Locos:** 3
Info/Talking Timetable: (0871) 222-1568	**N⁰ of Members:** 350
Year Formed: 1969	**Annual Membership Fee:** £14.00
Location of Line: North of Sittingbourne	**Approx N⁰ of Visitors P.A.:** 6,500
Length of Line: 2 miles	**Gauge:** 2 feet 6 inches
	Web site: www.sklr.net

GENERAL INFORMATION

Nearest Mainline Station: Sittingbourne (¼ mile)
Nearest Bus Station: Sittingbourne Mainline station
Car Parking: Sittingbourne Retail Park (behind McDonalds)
Coach Parking: Sittingbourne Retail Park
Souvenir Shop(s): Yes
Food & Drinks: Yes

SPECIAL INFORMATION

The railway is the only original preserved narrow gauge industrial steam railway in S.E. England (formerly the Bowaters Paper Company Railway). The railway celebrated 100 years of Steam locomotion in 2005 and the line includes a trip along a ½ mile concrete viaduct. Other attractions include a Museum, Model Railways, a Children's play area and a Wildlife Garden.

OPERATING INFORMATION

Opening Times: Sundays and Bank Holiday weekends from April to September. Also open on Wednesdays in the School holidays and for Santa Specials on certain dates in December. Phone for details of Special Events held throughout the year.
Steam Working: Trains run from 1.00pm normally, but from 11.00am on Bank Holiday weekends and Sundays in August. Last train runs at 4.00pm (except for during some special events).
Prices: Adult Return £5.00   Child Return £2.50   Senior Citizen Return £3.50   Family Return £14.00

Detailed Directions by Car:
From East or West: Take the M2 (or M20) to A249 and travel towards Sittingbourne. Take the A2 to Sittingbourne town and continue to the roundabout outside the Mainline station. Take the turning onto the B2006 (Milton Regis) under the Mainline bridge and the car park entrance for the Railway is by the next roundabout, behind McDonalds, in the Sittingbourne Retail Park.

SNOWDON MOUNTAIN RAILWAY

Address: Llanberis, Caernarfon, Gwynedd, Wales   LL55 4TY
Telephone Nº: (0870) 458-0033
Fax Nº: (01286) 872518
Year Formed: 1894
Location of Line: Llanberis to Snowdon summit

Length of Line: 4¾ miles
Nº of Steam Locos: 4
Nº of Other Locos: 4
Nº of Members: –
Approx Nº of Visitors P.A.: 140,000
Gauge: 2 feet 7½ inches
Web site: www.snowdonrailway.co.uk

GENERAL INFORMATION

Nearest Mainline Station: Bangor (9 miles)
Nearest Bus Station: Caernarfon (7½ miles)
Car Parking: Llanberis Station car park – pay and display. Also other car parks nearby.
Coach Parking: As above but space is very limited at busy times.
Souvenir Shop(s): Yes
Food & Drinks: Yes

SPECIAL INFORMATION

Britain's only public rack and pinion mountain railway. Climbs over 3,000 feet to Snowdon summit. Round trip approximately 2½ hours. From mid-March to early-May, the final section to the summit is closed and trains terminate lower down the mountain. Reduced fares then apply. Take a coat!

OPERATING INFORMATION

Opening Times: Open daily (weather permitting) from mid-March to the first week of November. Trains run from 9.00am until mid/late afternoon, subject to passenger demand.
Steam Working: Normally at least one steam loco on passenger service, but not guaranteed early or late in the season.
Prices: Adult £21.00   Child £14.00
Special rates are available for groups of 15 or more people.

Detailed Directions by Car:
Llanberis Station is situated on the A4086 Caernarfon to Capel Curig road, 7½ miles from Caernarfon. Convenient access via the main North Wales coast road (A55). Exit at the A55/A5 junction and follow signs to Llanberis via B4366, B4547 and A4086.

SOUTH DOWNS LIGHT RAILWAY

Address: South Downs Light Railway, Stopham Road, Pulborough RH20 1DS	**N° of Steam Locos**: 10
	N° of Other Locos: 3
Telephone N°: (07711) 717470	**N° of Members**: 50
Year Formed: 1999	**Annual Membership Fee**: Adult £20.00
Location: Pulborough Garden Centre	**Approx N° of Visitors P.A.**: 14,000
Length of Line: ½ mile	**Gauge**: 10¼ inches

GENERAL INFORMATION

Nearest Mainline Station: Pulborough (½ mile)
Nearest Bus Station: Bus stop just outside Centre
Car Parking: Free parking on site
Coach Parking: Free parking on site
Souvenir Shop(s): Yes
Food & Drinks: Yes – in the Garden Restaurant

SPECIAL INFORMATION

The members of the Society own and operate the largest collection of 10¼ inch gauge scale locomotives in the UK. The Railway is sited in the Pulborough Garden Centre.

OPERATING INFORMATION

Opening Times: Weekends and Bank Holidays from March until mid-September. Trains run from 11.00am to 3.30pm.
Steam Working: All services are steam hauled.
Prices: Adult £1.20
Child 80p
Under 3s travel free of charge.
Supersaver ticket provides 12 rides for the price of 10.

Web site: www.sdlrs.com

Detailed Directions by Car:
From All Parts: The Centre is situated on the A283, ½ mile west of Pulborough. Pulborough itself is on the A29 London to Bognor Regis Road.

SOUTH TYNEDALE RAILWAY

Address: The Railway Station, Alston, Cumbria CA9 3JB **Telephone Nº:** (01434) 381696 (Enquiries) (01434) 382828 (Talking timetable) **Year Formed:** 1973 **Location of Line:** From Alston, northwards along South Tyne Valley to Kirkhaugh	**Length of Line:** 2¼ miles **Nº of Steam Locos:** 5 **Nº of Other Locos:** 5 **Nº of Members:** 290 **Annual Membership Fee:** £15.00 **Approx Nº of Visitors P.A.:** 22,000 **Gauge:** 2 feet

GENERAL INFORMATION

Nearest Mainline Station: Haltwhistle (15 miles)
Nearest Bus Station: Alston Townfoot (¼ mile)
Car Parking: Free parking at Alston Station
Coach Parking: Free parking at Alston Station
Souvenir Shop(s): Yes
Food & Drinks: Yes

Web site: www.strps.org.uk

OPERATING INFORMATION

Opening Times: Bank Holidays and Weekends from 1st April until the end of October. Open daily from 17th July to 1st September. Also open Tuesday to Thursday in July and some other days in April, May, June, September, October and December – contact the Railway for further details.
Steam Working: Varies, but generally weekends and Bank Holidays throughout Summer & December. Also daily from 17th July to 1st September.
Prices: Adult Return £5.00; Adult Single £3.00
Child Return £2.50; Child Single £1.50
Children under 3 travel free
Adult All Day Ticket £8.00
Child All Day Ticket £3.00
Family All Day Ticket £14.00

Detailed Directions by Car:
Alston can be reached by a number of roads from various directions including A689, A686 and the B6277. Alston Station is situated just off the A686 Hexham road, north of Alston Town Centre. Look for the brown tourist signs on roads into Alston.

STAPLEFORD MINIATURE RAILWAY

Address: Stapleford Park, Stapleford, Melton Mowbray, Leicestershire
Telephone N°: (01949) 860138
Year Formed: 1957
Location of Line: Stapleford Park
Length of Line: 2 miles
Web site: www.fsmr.org.uk

N° of Steam Locos: 5
N° of Other Locos: 1
N° of Members: 45
Annual Membership Fee: By invitation
Approx N° of Visitors P.A.: Not known
Gauge: 10¼ inches

GENERAL INFORMATION

Nearest Mainline Station: Melton Mowbray (4 miles)
Nearest Bus Station: Melton Mowbray (4 miles)
Car Parking: Available on site
Coach Parking: Available on site
Souvenir Shop(s): Yes
Food & Drinks: Available – including a licensed bar

SPECIAL INFORMATION

The railway is only open to the public for two weekends a year as shown. The June event is run in conjunction with a Steam Rally and various traction engines will be on site. The August event concentrates on the railway with other smaller attractions. Weekend camping is available at both events. Please check the web site for details.

OPERATING INFORMATION

Opening Times: 17th/18th June 2006 and 27th/28th August 2006.
Steam Working: All trains on the open weekends
Prices: Adult Return £2.50
Child Return £1.50
Note: Family Tickets are also available

Detailed Directions by Car:
The railway is located off the B676 Melton Mowbray to Colsterworth road about 4 miles to the East of Melton Mowbray. The Stapleford Park Hotel is well-signposted with brown tourist signs and follow these to turn off the B676. The railway is located on the left hand side just before Stapleford Village and the turn into the hotel.

STEEPLE GRANGE LIGHT RAILWAY

Contact Address: 4 Oak Tree Gardens, Tansley, Matlock DE4 5WA
Telephone Nº: (01629) 580917
Year Formed: 1988
Location of Line: Off the High Peak trail near Wirksworth
Length of Line: ½ mile at present

Nº of Steam Locos: 1 (awaiting rebuild)
Nº of Other Locos: 17
Nº of Members: 120
Annual Membership Fee: From £5.00
Approx Nº of Visitors P.A.: 8,000+
Gauge: 18 inches
Web site: www.steeplegrange.co.uk

GENERAL INFORMATION

Nearest Mainline Station: Cromford (2 miles)
Nearest Bus Station: Matlock
Car Parking: Free parking available nearby
Coach Parking: Free parking available nearby
Souvenir Shop(s): Yes
Food & Drinks: Light refreshments available

SPECIAL INFORMATION

The Railway is built on the track bed of the former Standard Gauge Cromford and High Peak Railway branch to Middleton. The railway uses mostly former mining/quarrying rolling stock.

OPERATING INFORMATION

Opening Times: Sundays and Bank Holidays from Easter until the end of October. Also open on Saturdays from July to September and by prior arrangement. Special Events at other times of the year including Santa Specials on the 2nd weekend in December. Trains run from 12.00pm to 5.00pm
Steam Working: None at present
Prices: Adult Return £1.00
Child Return 50p
Note: Half-price fares are available for passengers with valid bus/train tickets. Special fares apply during special events and also for group bookings.

Detailed Directions by Car:
The Railway is situated adjacent to the National Stone Centre just to the north of Wirksworth at the junction of the B5035 and B5036. Free car parking is available at the National Stone Centre and in Old Porter Lane.

SUMMERFIELD FARM RAILWAY

Address: Summerfield Farm, Haynes, Bedford
Telephone Nº: (01234) 301867
Year Formed: 1992
Location: Off the A600, North of Haynes
Length of Line: Approximately ¾ mile
Web site: www.bmes.org.uk

Nº of Steam Locos: 8
Nº of Other Locos: 7
Nº of Members: Approximately 200
Annual Membership Fee: £20.00
Approx Nº of Visitors P.A.: 10,000
Gauge: 7¼ inches

GENERAL INFORMATION

Nearest Mainline Station: Bedford (5½ miles)
Nearest Bus Station: Bedford
Car Parking: Available on site
Coach Parking: Available on site
Souvenir Shop(s): None
Food & Drinks: Available

SPECIAL INFORMATION

Summerfield Farm Railway is operated by the Bedford Model Engineering Society.

OPERATING INFORMATION

Opening Times: Opening times vary – please phone for details.
Steam Working: On all public running days
Prices: Adult Return £1.50
Child Return £1.50

Detailed Directions by Car:
From All Parts: The Railway is located by the A600 just to the North of Haynes, 5½ miles South of Bedford and 3½ miles North of Shefford.

SUTTON HALL RAILWAY

Address: Tabors Farm, Sutton Hall, Shopland Road, near Rochford, Essex
Telephone Nº: (01702) 334337
Year Formed: 1997
Location of Line: Sutton Hall Farm
Length of Line: Almost 1 mile
Web site: uk.geocities.com/suttonrail

Nº of Steam Locos: 1
Nº of Other Locos: 1
Nº of Members: Approximately 8
Annual Membership Fee: £15.00
Approx Nº of Visitors P.A.: 3,500
Gauge: 10¼ inches

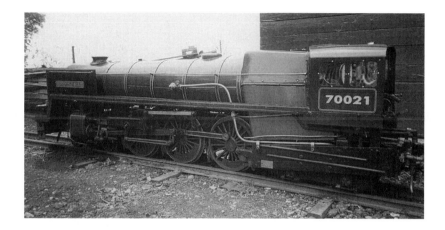

GENERAL INFORMATION

Nearest Mainline Station: Rochford (1½ miles)
Nearest Bus Station: Rochford
Car Parking: Free parking available on site
Coach Parking: Free parking available on site
Souvenir Shop(s): None
Food & Drinks: Drinks and snacks available

SPECIAL INFORMATION

The Railway was bought by C. Tabor in 1985 for use with his Farm Barn Dances. The Sutton Hall Railway Society was formed in 1997 (with C. Tabor as Society President) and now opens the line for public running on some Sundays. The railway is staffed entirely by Volunteer Members of the Society.

OPERATING INFORMATION

Opening Times: Open the 4th Sunday in the month from April until September, 12.00pm to 6.00pm. Specials run on Easter Sunday afternoon, Halloween evening and a Santa Special the 2nd Sunday afternoon in December.
Steam Working: All running days
Prices: Adult Return £2.00
Child Return £1.50

Detailed Directions by Car:
From Southend Airport (A127 Southend to London Main Route & A1158): At the Airport Roundabout (with the McDonalds on the left) go over the railway bridge signposted for Rochford. At the 1st roundabout turn right (Ann Boleyn Pub on the right) into Sutton Road. Continue straight on at the mini-roundabout then when the road forks turn left into Shopland Road signposted for Barling and Great Wakering. Turn right after approximately 400 yards into the long tree-lined road for Sutton Hall Farm.

TALYLLYN RAILWAY

Address: Wharf Station, Tywyn, Gwynedd, LL36 9EY
Telephone Nº: (01654) 710472
Year Formed: 1865
Location of Line: Tywyn to Nant Gwernol Station
Length of Line: 7¼ miles

Nº of Steam Locos: 6
Nº of Other Locos: 4
Nº of Members: 3,500
Annual Membership Fee: Adult £25.00
Approx Nº of Visitors P.A.: 50,000
Gauge: 2 feet 3 inches
Web site: www.talyllyn.co.uk

GENERAL INFORMATION

Nearest Mainline Station: Tywyn (300 yards)
Nearest Bus Station: Tywyn (300 yards)
Car Parking: 100 yards away
Coach Parking: Free parking (100 yards)
Souvenir Shop(s): Yes
Food & Drinks: Yes

SPECIAL INFORMATION

Talyllyn Railway was the first preserved railway in the world – saved from closure in 1951. The railway was opened in 1866 to carry slate from Bryn Eglwys Quarry to Tywyn.

OPERATING INFORMATION

Opening Times: Daily from 26th March to 4th November. Generally open from 10.00am to 5.00pm (later during the summer). Also open for Santa/New Year Specials on some dates in December/January.
Steam Working: All services are steam-hauled.
Prices: Adult Return £11.00 (Day Rover ticket) Children (ages 5-15) pay £2.00 if travelling with an adult. Otherwise, they pay half adult fare. Children under the age of 5 travel free of charge.
The fares shown above are for a full round trip. Tickets to intermediate stations are cheaper.

Detailed Directions by Car:
From the North: Take the A493 from Dolgellau into Tywyn; From the South: Take the A493 from Machynlleth to Tywyn.

TEIFI VALLEY RAILWAY

Address: Henllan Station, Henllan, near Newcastle Emlyn, Carmarthenshire	**N° of Steam Locos**: 2
	N° of Other Locos: 3
Telephone N°: (01559) 371077	**N° of Members**: Approximately 150
Year Formed: 1972	**Annual Membership Fee**: £12.00
Location of Line: Between Cardigan and Carmarthen off the A484	**Approx N° of Visitors P.A.**: 15,000
	Gauge: 2 feet
Length of Line: 2 miles	**Web site**: www.teifivalleyrailway.co.uk

GENERAL INFORMATION

Nearest Mainline Station: Carmarthen (10 miles)
Nearest Bus Station: Carmarthen (10 miles)
Car Parking: Spaces for 70 cars available.
Coach Parking: Spaces for 4 coaches available.
Souvenir Shop(s): Yes
Food & Drinks: Yes (snacks only)

SPECIAL INFORMATION

The Railway was formerly part of the G.W.R. but now runs on a Narrow Gauge using Quarry Engines.

OPERATING INFORMATION

Opening Times: Open daily from 25th March until the end of October (closed some Thursdays and Fridays). Also open on some days in December for 'Santa Specials'. Trains run from 11.00am – 4.30pm.
Steam Working: Occasional steam working – please phone the Railway for further details.
Prices: Adult £5.00
    Child £3.00
    Senio Citizens £4.50
A 10% discount is available for parties of 10 or more.

Detailed Directions by Car:
From All Parts: The Railway is situated in the Village of Henllan between the A484 and the A475 (on the B4334) about 4 miles east of Newcastle Emlyn.

THORNES PARK MINIATURE RAILWAY

Address: Thornes Park, Lawefield Lane, Wakefield, West Yorkshire **Telephone N°**: (01522) 800954 (Secretary) **Year Formed**: 1952 **Location**: Thornes Park, Wakefield **Length of Line**: ½ mile	**N° of Steam Locos**: 7 **N° of Other Locos**: 4 **N° of Members**: 35 **Annual Membership Fee**: £3.00 **Approx N° of Visitors P.A.**: 45,000 **Gauges**: 7¼ inches and 5 inches

GENERAL INFORMATION

Nearest Mainline Station: Wakefield Westgate (¾ mile)
Nearest Bus Station: Wakefield (1¼ miles)
Car Parking: Available on site
Coach Parking: Available on site
Souvenir Shop(s): None
Food & Drinks: None

SPECIAL INFORMATION

The railway is operated by members of the Wakefield Society of Model and Experimental Engineers. The group is non-profit making and all proceeds after operating costs are donated annually to the Mayor of Wakefield's chosen charity.

OPERATING INFORMATION

Opening Times: Sundays from Easter to October plus Saturdays and Bank Holidays depending on availability of manpower. Trains run from 1.00pm to 5.00pm. Also open for some other special events. Operation is dependent on weather conditions.
Steam Working: Generally whenever the railway is operating.
Prices: Adults 20p
Children 20p (free of charge for infants)

Detailed Directions by Car:
From All Parts: Thornes Park is located approximately 2 miles from Wakefield City Centre, just off the main Huddersfield to Wakefield road (A638).

VALE OF RHEIDOL RAILWAY

Address: The Locomotive Shed, Park Avenue, Aberystwyth, Dyfed SY23 1PG **Telephone Nº**: (01970) 625819 **Year Formed**: 1902 **Location of Line**: Aberystwyth to Devil's Bridge **Length of Line**: 11¾ miles	**Nº of Steam Locos**: 3 **Nº of Other Locos**: 1 **Nº of Members**: None **Annual Membership Fee**: – **Approx Nº of Visitors P.A.**: 38,000 **Gauge**: 1 foot 11¾ inches **Web site**: www.rheidolrailway.co.uk

GENERAL INFORMATION

Nearest Mainline Station: Aberystwyth (adjacent)
Nearest Bus Station: Aberystwyth (adjacent)
Car Parking: Available on site
Coach Parking: Parking available 400 yards away
Souvenir Shop(s): Yes
Food & Drinks: Yes

SPECIAL INFORMATION

The journey between the stations take one hour in each direction. At Devil's Bridge there is a cafe, toilets, a picnic area and the famous Mynach Falls. The line climbs over 600 feet in 11¾ miles.

OPERATING INFORMATION

Opening Times: Open almost every day from 14th April to 28th October with some exceptions. Please phone the railway for further information.
Steam Working: All trains are steam-hauled. Trains run from 10.30am to 4.00pm on most days.
Prices: Adult Return £12.50
Child Return – First 2 children per adult pay £3.00 each. Further children pay £6.25 each

Detailed Directions by Car:
From the North take A487 into Aberystwyth. From the East take A470 and A44 to Aberystwyth. From the South take A487 or A485 to Aberystwyth. The Station is joined on to the Mainline Station in Alexandra Road.

VANSTONE PARK MINIATURE RAILWAY

Address: Vanstone Park Garden Centre,
Hitchin Road, near Codicote SG4 8TH
Telephone Nº: (01438) 820412
Year Formed: 1986
Location: Vanstone Park Garden Centre
Length of Line: 600 yards

Nº of Steam Locos: None
Nº of Other Locos: 3
Nº of Members: None
Approx Nº of Visitors P.A.: Not known
Gauge: 10¼ inches
Web site: homepage.ntlworld.com/
antony.everett/vwr/

GENERAL INFORMATION

Nearest Mainline Station: Knebworth
Nearest Bus Station: Hitchin
Car Parking: Available on site
Coach Parking: Available on site
Souvenir Shop(s): Yes
Food & Drinks: Yes

SPECIAL INFORMATION

The Railway runs through the Vanstone Park
Garden Centre.

OPERATING INFORMATION

Opening Times: Weekends and Bank Holidays
throughout the year, weather permitting. Please
phone to avoid disappointment. Trains run from
11.00am to 4.30pm
Steam Working: None
Prices: Adult Return £1.40
Child Return £1.00

Detailed Directions by Car:
From All Parts: Exit the A1(M) at Junction 6 and take the B656. Vanstone Park is just off the B656 one mile to the
north of Codicote.

WATERWORKS RAILWAY

Address: Kew Bridge Steam Museum, Green Dragon Lane, Brentford TW8 0EN	**Nº of Steam Locos**: 1
Telephone Nº: (020) 8568-4757	**Nº of Other Locos**: 1
Year Formed: 1986	**Nº of Members**: 650
Location of Line: Greater London	**Annual Membership Fee**: £20.00 Adult
Length of Line: Under 1 mile	**Approx Nº of Visitors P.A.**: 20,000
	Gauge: Narrow

GENERAL INFORMATION

Nearest Mainline Station: Kew Bridge (3 minute walk)
Nearest Bus Station: Bus stop across the road – Services 65, 267 and 237
Car Parking: Spaces for 50 cars available on site
Coach Parking: Available on site – book in advance
Souvenir Shop(s): Yes
Food & Drinks: Yes – at weekends only

SPECIAL INFORMATION

The Museum is a former Victorian Pumping Station with a collection of working Steam Pumping Engines. The Railway demonstrates typical water board use of Railways.

OPERATING INFORMATION

Opening Times: 11.00am to 5.00pm, 7 days a week throughout the year.
Steam Working: Sundays and Bank Holiday Mondays from March to November.
Prices: Adult £6.50
            Child – Free if accompanied by Adults
            Senior Citizen £5.50

Web site: www.kbsm.org

Detailed Directions by Car:
From All Parts: Exit the M4 at Junction 2 and follow the A4 to Chiswick Roundabout. Take the exit signposted for Kew Gardens & Brentford. Go straight on at the next two sets of traffic lights following A315. After 2nd set of lights take the first right for the museum. The museum is next to the tall Victorian tower.

WELLS HARBOUR RAILWAY

Address: Wells Harbour Railway, Beach Road, Wells-next-the-Sea NR23 1DR **Telephone Nº**: (07939) 149264 **Year Formed**: 1976 **Location of Line**: Wells-next-the-Sea **Length of Line**: Approximately 1 mile	**Nº of Steam Locos**: 1 **Nº of Other Locos**: 2 **Nº of Members**: None **Approx Nº of Visitors P.A.**: 50,000 **Gauge**: 10¼ inches **Web site**: www.wellsharbourrailway.com

GENERAL INFORMATION

Nearest Mainline Station: King's Lynn (21 miles)
Nearest Bus Station: Norwich (24 miles)
Car Parking: Public car parks near each station
Coach Parking: Available in town
Souvenir Shop(s): No
Food & Drinks: No

SPECIAL INFORMATION

Wells Harbour Railway was the first 10¼" narrow gauge railway to run a scheduled passenger service and is listed in the Guinness Book of Records!

OPERATING INFORMATION

Opening Times: Weekends from Easter until Spring Bank Holiday then daily through to the middle of September. Then weekends until the end of October. The first train departs at 10.30am.
Steam Working: None
Prices: Adult Single £1.00
Child Single 70p

Detailed Directions by Car:
Wells-next-the-Sea is located on the North Norfolk cost between Hunstanton and Cromer. The railway is situated on Beach Road next to the harbour. Follow the signs for Pinewoods and Beach.

WELLS & WALSINGHAM LIGHT RAILWAY

Address: The Station, Wells-next-the-Sea NR23 1QB
Telephone Nº: (01328) 711630
Year Formed: 1982
Location of Line: Wells-next-the-Sea to Walsingham, Norfolk
Length of Line: 4 miles

Nº of Steam Locos: 1
Nº of Other Locos: 2
Nº of Members: 50
Annual Membership Fee: £11.00
Approx Nº of Visitors P.A.: 20,000
Gauge: 10¼ inches

GENERAL INFORMATION

Nearest Mainline Station: King's Lynn (21 miles)
Nearest Bus Station: Norwich (24 miles)
Car Parking: Free parking at site
Coach Parking: Free parking at site
Souvenir Shop(s): Yes
Food & Drinks: Yes

SPECIAL INFORMATION

The Railway is the longest 10¼ inch narrow-gauge steam railway in the world. The course of the railway is famous for wildlife and butterflies in season.

OPERATING INFORMATION

Opening Times: Daily from 1st April until the end of October.
Steam Working: Trains run from 10.15am on operating days.
Prices: Adult Return £7.00
Child Return £5.50

Detailed Directions by Car:
Wells-next-the-Sea is situated on the North Norfolk Coast midway between Hunstanton and Cromer. The Main Station is situated on the main A149 Stiffkey Road. Follow the brown tourist signs for the Railway.

WELSH HIGHLAND RAILWAY (CAERNARFON)

Postal Address: Ffestiniog Railway,
Harbour Station, Porthmadog LL49 9NF
Telephone Nº: (01766) 516000
Web site: www.festrail.co.uk
Year Formed: 1997
Location: Caernarfon to Rhyd Ddu
Length of Line: 12 miles

Nº of Steam Locos: 5 (2 working)
Nº of Other Locos: 2
Nº of Members: 1,000
Annual Membership Fee: £25.00
Approx Nº of Visitors P.A.: 50,000
Gauge: 1 foot 11½ inches
Web site: www.festrail.co.uk

GENERAL INFORMATION

Nearest Mainline Station: Bangor (7 miles) (Bus
service Nº 5 runs to Caernarfon)
Nearest Bus Station: Caernarfon
Car Parking: Parking available at Caernarfon
Coach Parking: At Victoria Docks (¼ mile)
Souvenir Shop(s): Yes
Food & Drinks: Light refreshments on some trains

SPECIAL INFORMATION

The Railway is being reconstructed between
Caernarfon and Porthmadog along the track bed of
the original Welsh Highland Railway. Please check
the Railway web site for up to date information.

OPERATING INFORMATION

Opening Times: Daily from 9th April to 5th
November but closed on some Mondays and Fridays
in October. Train times vary.
Steam Working: Most trains in the Summer are
steam-hauled.
Prices: Adult Day Rover £18.50
Child Day Rover £8.25
Senior Citizen Day Rover £13.20
Note: One Child is admitted free of charge with
every paying Adult. Also, price reductions are
available for groups of 20 or more.

Detailed Directions by Car:
Take either the A487(T), the A4085 or the A4086 to Caernarfon then follow the brown tourist signs for the
Railway which is situated in St. Helens Road next to the Castle.

WELSH HIGHLAND RAILWAY (PORTHMADOG)

Address: Tremadog Road, Porthmadog, Gwynedd LL49 9DY	**Nº of Steam Locos:** 6
Telephone Nº: (01766) 513402	**Nº of Other Locos:** 20
Year Formed: 1964	**Nº of Members:** 1,000
Location of Line: Porthmadog,	**Annual Membership Fee:** £25.00 Adult
Gwynedd LL49 9DY	**Approx Nº of Visitors P.A.:** 15,858 (2005)
Length of Line: ¾ mile	**Gauge:** 1 foot 11½ inches
	Web site: www.whr.co.uk

GENERAL INFORMATION

Nearest Mainline Station: Porthmadog (50 yards)
Nearest Bus Station: Services 1 & 3 stop 200 yards away
Car Parking: Free parking at site, plus a public car park within 100 yards
Coach Parking: Adjacent
Souvenir Shop(s): Yes – large range available.
Food & Drinks: Yes – excellent home cooking!

SPECIAL INFORMATION

The Welsh Highland Railway is a family-orientated attraction based around a Railway Heritage Centre and includes a tour of the sheds. A ½ mile extension to Traeth Mawr is expected to open in 2006.

OPERATING INFORMATION

Opening Times: Daily from 8th April to 1st October; 7/8/14/15/21-29 October. Trains run at 10.45am, 11.45am, 1.30pm, 2.30pm, 3.30pm and 4.30pm (the last train runs at 3.30pm during September/October).
Steam Working: 15-23/29/30 April; 1/27-31 May; 1-4 June; 22-31 July; 1-28 August; 2/3/9/10/16/17/ 23/24 September; 21-29 October.
Prices: Adult Return £4.95   Child Return £2.95
        Senior Citizen Return £3.95
        Family Return £13.95
        (2 adults + 2 children)
Children under 5 are admitted free of charge

Detailed Directions by Car:
From Bangor/Caernarfon take the A487 to Porthmadog. From Pwllheli take the A497 to Porthmadog then turn left at the roundabout. From the Midlands take A487 to Portmadog. Once in Porthmadog, follow the brown tourist signs. The line is located right next to Porthmadog Mainline Station.

WELSHPOOL & LLANFAIR LIGHT RAILWAY

Address: The Station, Llanfair Caereinion, Powys SY21 0SF	**Nº of Steam Locos:** 9
Telephone Nº: (01938) 810441	**Nº of Other Locos:** 4
Year Formed: 1959	**Nº of Members:** 2,300
Location of Line: Welshpool to Llanfair Caereinion, Mid Wales	**Annual Membership Fee:** £22.50
	Approx Nº of Visitors P.A.: 25,000
Length of Line: 8 miles	**Gauge:** 2 feet 6 inches
	Web site: www.wllr.org.uk

GENERAL INFORMATION

Nearest Mainline Station: Welshpool (1 mile)
Nearest Bus Station: Welshpool (1 mile)
Car Parking: Free parking at Welshpool and Llanfair Caereinion
Coach Parking: As above
Souvenir Shop(s): Yes – at both ends of line
Food & Drinks: Yes – at Llanfair only

SPECIAL INFORMATION

The railway has the steepest gradient of any British railway, reaching a summit of 603 feet.

OPERATING INFORMATION

Opening Times: Easter and Bank Holidays and weekends from 8th April to 29th October. Daily from 22nd July to 3rd September. Most other days in June and July plus dates in September, October and December. Generally open from 9.30am to 5.00pm.
Steam Working: All trains are steam-hauled
Prices: Adult £10.50
          Senior Citizens £9.50
Children under the age of 3 are free of charges. The first child aged 3-15 per adult also travels free. All other children are charged half-price fare of £5.25

Detailed Directions by Car:
Both stations are situated alongside the A458 Shrewsbury to Dolgellau road and are clearly signposted

---

WEST LANCASHIRE LIGHT RAILWAY

Address: Station Road, Hesketh Bank, Nr. Preston, Lancashire PR4 6SP **Telephone Nº**: (01772) 815881 **Year Formed**: 1967 **Location of Line**: On former site of Alty's Brickworks, Hesketh Bank **Length of Line**: ¼ mile	**Nº of Steam Locos**: 9 **Nº of Other Locos**: 24 **Nº of Members**: Approximately 95 **Annual Membership Fee**: £15.00 Adult; £20.00 Family **Approx Nº of Visitors P.A.**: 14,500 **Web site**: www.westlancs.org

GENERAL INFORMATION

Nearest Mainline Station: Rufford (4 miles)
Nearest Bus Station: Preston (7 miles)
Car Parking: Space for 50 cars at site
Coach Parking: Space for 3 coaches at site
Souvenir Shop(s): Yes
Food & Drinks: Only soft drinks & snacks

SPECIAL INFORMATION

The Railway is run by volunteers and there is a large collection of Industrial Narrow Gauge equipment.

OPERATING INFORMATION

Opening Times: Sundays and Bank Holidays throughout the year. No trains run from November to April (except Santa Specials). Various other Special Events are held during the Summer – phone for details or check the Railway's web site listed above. Trains run from 12.00pm to 5.20pm
Steam Working: Trains operate on Sundays and Bank Holidays from April until the end of October. There are also 'Santa Specials' on the two weekends prior to Christmas.
Prices: Adult £2.00   Child £1.25
            Family Tickets £4.50
            Senior Citizens £1.50

Detailed Directions by Car:
Travel by the A59 from Liverpool or Preston or by the A565 from Southport to the junction of the two roads at Tarleton. From here follow signs to Hesketh Bank. The Railway is signposted.

WESTON MINIATURE RAILWAY

Address: Marine Parade,
Weston-super-Mare, Somerset
Telephone Nº: (01934) 643510
Year Formed: 1981
Location of Line: Marine Parade
Length of Line: 900 yards
Web site: westonmr.tripod.com

Nº of Steam Locos: 1
Nº of Other Locos: 2
Nº of Members: None
Annual Membership Fee: –
Approx Nº of Visitors P.A.: 20,000
Gauge: 7¼ inches

GENERAL INFORMATION

Nearest Mainline Station: Weston-super-Mare
Nearest Bus Station: Weston-super-Mare
Car Parking: Available nearby on the seafront
Coach Parking: Available on the seafront
Souvenir Shop(s): Yes
Food & Drinks: Available

SPECIAL INFORMATION

This is a popular tourist railway running along the
Weston-super-Mare seafront.

OPERATING INFORMATION

Opening Times: Daily from Spring Bank Holiday
until September. Also open at weekends from
February to October.
Steam Working: Some Sundays.
Prices: Adult £1.50
Child £1.50

Detailed Directions by Car:
From All Parts: The Railway is situated at the Southern end of the seafront in Weston-super-Mare. Follow the
brown tourist signs

WINDMILL ANIMAL FARM RAILWAY

Address: Windmill Animal Farm, Red Cat Lane, Burscough L40 1UQ **Telephone Nº**: (07971) 221343 **Year Formed**: 1997 **Location of Line**: Burscough, Lancashire **Length of Line**: ¾ mile	**Nº of Steam Locos**: 5 **Nº of Other Locos**: 6 **Nº of Members**: 7 **Annual Membership Fee**: None **Approx Nº of Visitors P.A.**: 40,000 **Gauge**: 15 inches **Web**: www.windmillanimalfarm.co.uk

Photo courtesy of Chris Mansfield

GENERAL INFORMATION

Nearest Mainline Station: Burscough (2½ miles)
Nearest Bus Station: Southport (8½ miles)
Car Parking: Available at the Farm
Coach Parking: Available at the Farm
Souvenir Shop(s): Yes
Food & Drinks: Available

SPECIAL INFORMATION

In addition to the railway, the site includes a play area and a large number of farm animals with a petting area where children can feed the animals.

OPERATING INFORMATION

Opening Times: Open Daily from Easter until mid-September and during weekends and school holidays at all other times. 10.00am to 5.00pm.
Steam Working: Every weekend
Prices: Adult Admission £4.50
         Child Admission £3.75
Train Rides: Adult £1.50
         Child £1.00

Detailed Directions by Car:
From All Parts: Exit the M6 at Junction 27 and take the A5209 following signs for Southport. On entering Burscough follow signs for Burscough Bridge and Martin Lane. Turn left into Red Cat Lane just by Burscough Bridge train station and follow the road along for Windmill Animal Farm and the Railway.

WOKING MINIATURE RAILWAY

Address: Barrs Lane, Knaphill, Woking, Surrey   GU21 2JW
Telephone Nº: (01483) 720801
Year Formed: 1989
Location of Line: Knaphill, Surrey
Length of Line: 1 mile

Nº of Steam Locos: 10
Nº of Other Locos: 6
Nº of Members: 110
Annual Membership Fee: £15.00
Approx Nº of Visitors P.A.: 15,000
Gauge: 7¼ inches
Web site: www.mizensrailway.org.uk

GENERAL INFORMATION

Nearest Mainline Station: Woking
Nearest Bus Station: Woking
Car Parking: 200 spaces available on site
Coach Parking: Available on site
Souvenir Shop(s): Yes
Food & Drinks: Available on running days

SPECIAL INFORMATION

The Railway is situated in a beautiful location admist 8 acres of woodland. In addition to over a mile of track, the railway has three stations, two signalboxes, a tunnel, a Roundhouse Engine Shed, a level crossing and authentic buildings.

OPERATING INFORMATION

Opening Times: Easter Sunday then every Sunday from May to September. Trains run from 2.00pm to 5.00pm. Santa Specials run on Sundays in December from 11.00am to 3.00pm.
Steam Working: Most operating days
Prices: Adult Return £1.50 – £2.00
        Child Return £1.50 – £2.00

Detailed Directions by Car:
From All Parts: Exit the M25 at Junction 11 and follow the A320 to Woking. At the Six Cross Roads Roundabout take the 5th exit towards Knaphill then turn left at the roundabout onto Littlewick Road. Continue along Littlewick Road crossing the roundabout before turning right into Barrs Lane just before Knaphill.

WORTLEY TOP FORGE MINIATURE RAILWAY

Contact Address: 3 Grange Road, Royston, Barnsley   S71 4LD
Telephone No: (01226) 728423
Year Formed: Not known
Location of Line: Top Forge, Wortley near Thurgoland in Sheffield
Length of Line: ¼ mile

No of Steam Locos: Varies
No of Other Locos: Varies
No of Members: Approximately 60
Annual Membership Fee: £15.00
Approx No of Visitors P.A.: Not known
Gauges: 7¼ inches and 5 inches
Web site: www.wortleymes.com

GENERAL INFORMATION

Nearest Mainline Station: Barnsley or Sheffield
Nearest Bus Station: Barnsley
Car Parking: Available on site
Coach Parking: Available on site
Souvenir Shop(s): None
Food & Drinks: Available in the Club house

SPECIAL INFORMATION

The railway is owned by the Wortley Top Forge Model Engineers Society and runs through the grounds of the Wortley Top Forge industrial museum.

OPERATING INFORMATION

Opening Times: Sunday afternoons from Easter until November.
Steam Working: Most operating days.
Prices: Donations are accepted

Detailed Directions by Car:
Wortley Top Forge is situated within 10 minutes drive of the M1 motorway. From the South: Exit the M1 at Junction 35A and follow the A616 then A629 to Thurgoland; From the North: Exit the M1 at Junction 36 and follow the A61 then A616 and finally the A629 to Thurgoland. Once in Thurgoland, the forge site is ½ mile to the west of the traffic lights in the centre of the village.

ALSO AVAILABLE –

STILL STEAMING
– A Guide To
Britain's Standard Gauge
Steam Railways
2006/2007

£6.99

The new 10th edition of **Still Steaming** is packed with information about Britain's top Standard-gauge Railways and includes –

• **PHOTOS** • **DIRECTIONS** • **FARES** • **STEAMING DATES** • **CONTACT INFO**

…and much more. *Priced just £6.99* (UK post free)

Order from:

Marksman Publications, 72 St. Peters Avenue, Cleethorpes, DN35 8HU

Telephone (01472) 696226 Fax (01472) 698546 www.stillsteaming.com